IT'S YOUR TURN
TO BE BLESSED

ABOUT THE AUTHOR. . .DR. C. S. LOVETT

Dr. Lovett is the president of **Personal Christianity Chapel,** a fundamental, evangelical interdenominational ministry. For the past 34 years he has had but one objective — **preparing Christians for the second coming of Christ!** This book is one of over 40 of his works designed to help believers **prepare for His appearing.**

Dr. Lovett's decision to serve the Lord resulted in the loss of a sizable personal fortune. He is well equipped for the job the Lord has given him. A graduate of American Baptist Seminary of the West, he holds the M.A. and M.Div. degrees conferred *Magna Cum Laude.* He has also completed graduate work in psychology at Los Angeles State College and holds an honorary doctorate from the Protestant Episcopal University in London.

A retired Air Force Chaplain (Lt. Colonel), he has been married to Marjorie for over 42 years and has two grown daughters dedicated to the Lord.

IT'S YOUR TURN TO BE BLESSED

C. S. LOVETT

M.A., M. Div., D.D.

president of Personal Christianity Chapel

author of fifteen best selling books including:
Latest Word on the Last Days
Dealing With The Devil
Soul-Winning Made Easy
"Help Lord — The Devil Wants Me Fat!"

editorial assistance
by Linda Lovett

published by:
PERSONAL CHRISTIANITY CHAPEL
Box 549
Baldwin Park, California 91706

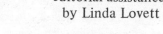

MY THANKS TO FRANK HUTCHINSON

Who started my thinking about our small
sins and how they add up in God's sight.
His example challenged me to make a 100%
commitment to try to overcome them, and
share the know-how with others.

PRINTED IN THE UNITED STATES OF AMERICA
ISBN 0-938148-39-7

Contents

Introduction — **There Shall Be Showers of Blessing** . . . 6

PART ONE

Chapter one — **God Wants To Bless You** 11

Chapter Two — **How to Put Yourself
in The Place of Blessing** 35

PART TWO

Chapter Three — **Abiding in His Blessing** 58

Chapter Four — **Getting Involved in
What He's Doing** 85

In This Book 111

The Daily Prayer of A Committed Christian 112

Appendix — **Questions Frequently Asked** 113

Introduction

THERE SHALL BE
SHOWERS OF BLESSING

THE CHRISTIAN DREAM

After a person is saved and discovers he's a true child of God, it is natural for him to think his life will be blessed — AUTOMATICALLY. And if he goes to church regularly, prays often and tithes, he's even more convinced good things will come flowing into his life. After all, his Father is super rich, owning the "cattle on a thousand hills" (Psa. 50:10). Beyond that, he's been told he can ask ANYTHING in Jesus' name AND GET IT (John 14:13). He has every reason to be expectant.

So the believer fantasizes about the good things God is going to do for him. First he expects God to provide him with a nice home, a good job or career. Besides that, he's sure God is going to give him a healthy, happy family, all serving the Lord together. Then, on top of that, he looks for God to bless his body, his finances, even his desires. What Christian feels there is a limit to what God can shower on those He loves?

Ah, but do things work out that way? Rarely.

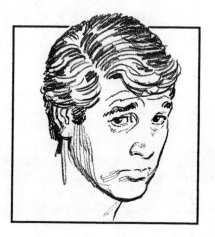

See the perplexed look on that fellow? There's no shower of blessings in his life. That's obvious. A few drops, perhaps, but no shower. Yet, he's a fairly solid Christian by today's standards. He's in church every Sunday and prays a lot, yet things aren't working out as he hoped. Things aren't all that good at home, lots of bickering. Rough at work, too. His kids travel with the wrong crowd. Even his neighbor fusses with him.

7

Then there are financial pressures. To make matters worse, his family seems to have its share of sickness.

Even the car gives him a bad time. Life is nowhere near what he thought it would be when he became deeply involved in the new life. Even church isn't that much fun any more. "I sure thought I could expect more from the Lord than this," he complains. "I see plenty of non-christians better off than I am."

There's a lot the Lord would LIKE TO DO for this man, BUT HIS HANDS ARE TIED. Our brother is not alone in his situation. The bulk of God's children are just like him and He can't bless them either. How come? **They're not in the place of blessing.** Until they BRING THEMSELVES to the place where God can shower His blessings on them, things have to remain as they are.

Of course God keeps hoping the pressures of life will SHAKE His children to the place where they'll ask, "WHAT'S WRONG?" But it doesn't seem to work that way. Most go day after day, year after year, experiencing disappointment and pain — and no real blessings.

Fortunately, not all do that.

8

"Hey!" says the thinking Christian, "there must be a reason why God's blessings aren't flowing in my life as they're supposed to. Maybe it's my fault. I know God loves me. I'm sure he WANTS to bless me, but . . .

"Hummmmh, maybe I'm not in the place where He can bless me.

"Well, if that's the case, I wonder what I can do about it?"

THAT'S WHAT THIS BOOK IS ALL ABOUT!

What you're about to read will show you how to put yourself in the **place of blessing.** But you'll have to make a commitment, I mean a real commitment that sees you making a sincere effort to please the Lord every moment of the day. If you'll do it, the blessings of God will flow in a torrent.

NOTE: This is not a program of GIVING TO GET. So please don't confuse it with radio and TV programs that ask you to send money in order to secure God's financial blessing. This is not that kind of approach. What you'll be asked to give IS YOURSELF. You'll be yielding yourself to God to PLEASE HIM, to bring Him joy. In doing so, you

9

UNTIE HIS HANDS so He can shower His blessings on you. He WANTS to do this. He ACHES to do it, as would any loving father. But He can only do it as a BY-PRODUCT of your putting Him first, or at least TRYING TO.

What you're about to learn is HOW TO STEP INTO the shower of God's blessing. He longs to bless and prosper you. In fact He's been wanting to do it for a long time. But how about you? Are you ready to yield yourself to Him? Are you ready for His best? We'll see.

THIS BOOK HAS TO DO WITH GETTING UNDER GOD'S SHOWER AND STAYING THERE. HE HAS BLESSINGS IN ABUNDANCE FOR ALL. HE HAS NO FAVORITES. HE IS NO RESPECTER OF PERSONS. HE LOVES YOU AS MUCH AS HE LOVES BILLY GRAHAM.

PART ONE

Chapter One

GOD WANTS TO BLESS YOU

"Set your mind on God's Kingdom . . . before every-thing else and all the rest will come to you as well."
(Matt. 6:33 NEB)

Ever wonder why you're on this earth? Why God made you? Why He created you the unique individual you are, with your abilities and weaknesses, your temperament and traits? Or what His purpose might be in putting you on earth at this time?

Well, GOD IS A FATHER, a "family man." He wanted children of His own. That's why He made you. He wanted those on whom He could shower His love and have it returned. So desperately did He want you, He sent Jesus to suffer and die that you might be able to DRAW CLOSE to Him. He longs for an "intimate family" relationship. He yearns to bless those who make it their ambition to get as close to Him as possible.

WORTH THE EFFORT

Anyone who'll make the effort to get close to our Father won't be sorry. He's so generous. He loves to give. He is the GREAT GIVER, for it is His nature to give. It thrills Him to shower His blessings on all who will let Him. The vast wealth of heaven means nothing to Him — without someone to share it. Sharing what He has with others is a passion with Him. To Him, giving is living! It pains Him when he **can't** give.

As He watches His children on earth, He burns with a desire to touch their lives with health, financial success and the best of family living. It thrills God when He can lavish super health on us, satisfying jobs, nice houses and godly children.

Here's a politician, for example, who has yielded himself to put God first. It is FUN for God to grant that man favor with the public, backing Him with over-whelming support. The people applaud his ideas and his financial coffers are full. Consider the businessman who is determined to give Jesus the highest priority in his life. God is delighted to draw people to His products with word-of-mouth favor that surpasses any advertising program. Such a man can't miss. God will see to it.

Then there's the godly homemaker who makes it her aim to please God first of all. The Lord will reward her by filling her heart with the greatest joy as she watches her family blossom under her anointed ministry. Her children love her and listen to her. Her husband adores her and lavishes sweet affection on her. Her friends can't get over the love and joy that fill her home. But they could have it too — if they would make the same commitment. When you set your heart to please God, His heart is already set to please yours.

Unfortunately, many of God's children are totally UNAWARE of His **longing to bless them,** and how it hurts Him when He can't. They're so busy with worldly routines they don't have time to check into His longings, let alone do anything about them. Others are simply indifferent. Regardless of the reason, they put themselves OUTSIDE THE SHOWER and deny Him what He longs for most. Any believer who wants a steady stream of good things from God MUST GET UNDER THE SHOWER.

WHAT DO WE HAVE TO DO?

If God created us for INTIMACY and BLESSING, how do we go about getting them? How do we get under the shower?

There are two things we must do:

1. We must draw as close to the Lord as possible.

2. We must commit our lives to Him as fully as possible.

Here's what I'm talking about — yielding yourself COMPLETELY to Jesus with NO RESERVATION of any kind. You know, like He's done for you. He went all the way for you, withholding nothing. In giving His life on the cross, He gave all He had. This demands your putting forth your BEST EFFORT to please Him **in every area of your life.** You must TRY to make everything you DO, SAY, and THINK as pleasing to Him as possible — in absolutely everything.

IMPOSSIBLE, YOU SAY

You're right. It is — in the flesh. Our old natures (our fleshly drives), which are so powerful, don't want to please the Lord. We can't look to them for help, since they want only to please SELF. There's no way for the flesh to please God (Rom. 8:8). The old nature will FIGHT every attempt you make to please the Lord. And does that ever make for a battle. Wow!

The flesh WARS against the spirit, says the apostle Paul, and the spirit against the flesh. It is this WAR that makes it impossible to please God without help (Gal. 5:17). Ah, but we **do** have help. The Holy Spirit is eager to help us — **when our motive is right.** And here's the right motive. It has two parts:

FIRST: Because we truly love Jesus, we desire to make Him as happy as we can. We do this by yielding to His will — yes, even WANTING to do only that which is pleasing to Him (1st John 3:22; 1 Thess. 4:1).

SECOND: We have personal desires for success in those things we undertake in the world. We want to enjoy the good things of this life. We have ambitions concerning things we'd like to accomplish in this world. God knows we have such ambitions, and He's pleased that we do.

Sound inconsistent to find the DESIRE FOR SUCCESS a part of **proper motivation** for a Christian? Ah, don't forget: THIS IS WHAT GOD WANTS FOR US, TOO. He wants us to prosper in business and

14

enjoy good health — in fact, in EVERYTHING we do. He's ambitious, and we're His image. So when our motive is right, we can expect the Spirit's help with our personal ambitions. But we do have to keep things in the right order — putting **first things first.**

FIRST THINGS FIRST

Look again at the two elements of proper motivation. Which is first? The desire to make God happy by **yielding to His will** in everything. (Not in a legalistic way, for then we become like the Pharisees.) We do so because WE WANT TO. It gives us joy to make Him happy. Our first ambition is to be a blessing to Him. That's where we have to begin.

We can't start with our desire for success. That's selfish. You can't please anyone that way. Not your wife, not your husband. Certainly not God. That attitude puts us OUTSIDE THE SHOWER. No, we must not reverse the order. He has to be first.

NOT THE CART BEFORE THE HORSE

I was sharing this BLESSING CONCEPT with a friend. The Spirit backed the truth as I began telling her how EAGER God is to pour out His best, and how it is possible for her to be fully blessed every day.

When she grasped the significance of what I was saying, her eyes lit up.

"That's what I want," she exclaimed. "For the first time in my Christian life I feel the Holy Spirit telling me it is all right for a Christian to be successful and prosperous in this world."

She went away excited, realizing she'd found the

15

KEY TO SUCCESS. She just knew God was going to shower His blessings on her. But when I saw her six months later, this was her confession:

"After we talked that day, I went away on cloud nine. I was so thrilled to discover it was OK for believers to desire success, I guess it blinded me. I forgot the FIRST PART of our motivation. I had no thought of making a commitment or changing my life in any way. As a result, nothing happened. No blessings came my way."

" Then the Spirit led me to some Bible passages that teach us to expect blessings from God as a BY-PRODUCT OF PUTTING HIM FIRST. **That's what I had missed.** In my enthusiasm, I was putting my desires ahead of His. Oh, I did the normal things, like going to church and tithing and so on, but I certainly wasn't committing myself to the Lord totally. In fact, I wasn't even trying. I realize now, Dr. Lovett, I must yield everything to Him. I hate to confess this. BUT I DON'T KNOW HOW. Will you help me get started?"

Would I? Of course. Her request thrilled me. God too. So we began with God's own formula:

PUTTING THE LORD FIRST

 ". . . seek first His kingdon and His righteousness; and all these things shall be added to you."   — Matt. 6:33 NAS

This is the way Jesus summed up His Sermon on the Mount. Actually it is His formula for enjoying the blessings of His kingdom **here and now.** It's a promise. But behind that promise is His longing to have His children pay attention to Him and come to Him for His blessing. He has set things up so that there are NO

16

BLESSINGS when we exclude Him. He has to with-hold, or Christians will never bother with Him. **Tough, but that's the power of the flesh.**

God guarantees IN WRITING that His blessings will flow if we put Him first. Having never once failed in any of His promises, He will do as He says. All of heaven's resources are at His disposal. So all that is necessary is for us to do our part (putting Him first), and He will do His part (showering the blessings on us).

● But many will say:

"Look, I'm doing OK as a Christian. I don't see that I'm any different from other 'committed' Christians. I don't lie . . . cheat . . . steal . . . intentionally hurt others. Certainly I'm not involved in any of the BIG SINS. As far as I can tell, I've committed myself to the Lord as fully as the next guy. It's because of my commitment that I shun the big sins of life. So where could I be falling short?"

AH, IN THE LITTLE SINS

We've come to what many will regard as the most important contribution of this book. I want to draw your attention to the LITTLE SINS that literally **flood the life** of a "committed" Christian. And here's the surprise. When you ADD UP the tiny **disobediences,** and behold the total, that total is every bit as bad in the sight of God as any of the so-called BIG SINS. This applies to all of us — including C. S. Lovett.

When I first became aware of the LITTLE SINS concept, I took a hard look at my life. Sure enough, I had a closet full of things that added up to something awful in God's sight . . . things I'd say . . . things I'd think. Things I once considered of no interest to God now loomed as awful disappointments to Him. There was no way I could be truly pleasing to Him and that rocked me.

It was painful facing the truth I was secretly proud of the fact I didn't smoke, drink, eat harmful foods or commit adultery. I paid my bills promptly and went out of my way to defraud no one. I didn't even like to gossip. I took for granted I was a fairly decent Christian, particularly since I was so occupied with the Lord's work. I was busy at my typewriter hours each day, preaching every Sunday and shepherding my little flock. I didn't see how I could be too far out of God's will.

But when I summed up all my SMALL DISOBEDIENCES, THEY EASILY COMPARED TO THE MORE GROSS SINS.

I was sinning worse than I thought!
No wonder God couldn't shower His blessings on me!
How could He? I was outside the shower!

It wasn't until my dear friend, Frank Hutchinson, spoke to me concerning the LITTLE SINS, that I truly took note of them. The moment he mentioned them, the Spirit's witness was heavy. I looked all around my life to see if I could find them, and there they were, plenty of them.

I went to work on them, and as is usually the case with me, **a plan emerged**. When I went to the Lord about these small sins, He gladly showed me how to overcome them and be in the PLACE OF BLESSING. But He also made it clear I was not to keep the knowhow to myself.

So that's what you'll find in these pages, the plan the Lord gave. Frank and I have been using it successfully, and as a result, we're enjoying God's shower of blessing.

Not that He didn't bless us before, but there's a big difference between droplets and a shower.

DROPLETS VS SHOWERS

Why should any Christian be content with droplets of God's blessing, when He is eager to turn on the shower full force? Even the busiest of Christians limit themselves to a trickle if they do nothing about their small sins. It's a shame to live so far below our privileges in Christ when God WANTS to GIVE so much.

ABOUT THOSE LITTLE SINS

Let's zero in on them.

Just what are they specifically?

Whether we will admit it or not, there are areas in our lives where we insist on DOING OUR OWN THING, and in our own way. There are tiny disobediences which we don't look on as sin, nor do we think God pays any attention to them. But we fool ourselves, no, we deceive ourselves. God isn't fooled. He beholds every thought in our heads and the intentions of our hearts. He sees our motives and knows what's behind everything we do and think.

To God, all those little sins add up to **a mountain, a hideous mountain of sin.** Were He not such a gracious Father, He'd lower the boom on us. Instead, He withholds His blessing and allows tribulation to come our way. He wants to shake us up, discipline us (Heb. 12:5-8). Even then, His sole purpose is to make us aware of what we're doing. He wants us to see "Sin Mountain" and face up to **how UNCOMMITTED we really are.** We may think we're committed to Him, but that mountain says otherwise. God wants us to realize WE'RE OUT OF THE SHOWER and a long way from the 100% He asks for.

This is why He can't bless us as He yearns to. Instead, He has to send trials and testings on a continual basis — for as long as it takes to make us "wake up and smell the coffee."

● Let me mention some of those areas:

THOUGHTS . . . BODIES . . . TIME . . . MONEY . . . TALENTS . . . WORK

You can think of more, but I want to discuss these

just enough to show how they add up to something terrible in God's eyes, and put us outside the shower. You'll get the picture, I'm sure.

THOUGHTS

"The thought is father to the deed," said Emerson. "As a man thinketh in his heart, so is he," said Solomon. James was more precise:

 "But each one is tempted when he is carried away and enticed by his own lust (lust occurs in the mind). **Then when lust has CONCEIVED, it gives birth to sin . . . "**
— James 1:14,15 NAS

Sin occurs in the mind. Before an evil act is carried out in the flesh, it is first CONCEIVED in one's thought life, **and that's what God sees.** Old Samuel taught us: " . . . man looketh on the outward appearance, but the Lord LOOKETH ON THE HEART" (1 Sam. 16:7 KJV). Obviously, many acts that occur in the mind are never carried out in the flesh, often because there is no opportunity to do so. But they're just as offensive to God. Jesus explained that to us:

 "You have heard that it was said, 'YOU SHALL NOT COMMIT ADULTERY'; but I say to you, that everyone who looks on a woman to lust for her has committed adultery with her ALREADY in his heart."
— Matt. 5:27, 28 NAS

and again

"You have heard that the ancients were told, 'YOU SHALL NOT COMMIT MURDER' . . . But I say to you that everyone who is ANGRY with his brother shall be guilty ..."
— Matt. 5:21,22 NAS

The apostle John tells why that person is guilty:

 "Everyone who hates his brother is a MURDERER . . ." — 1st John 3:15 NAS

See, the mind is the place where we sin. If a person's mind is not DISCIPLINED, it can be a garbage dump. You know how easily our thoughts drift from scene to scene, like a bee going from flower to flower, with no control over them at all. This makes it easy for Satan to insert HIS IDEAS. As a result, he authors much, if not most, of the wickedness occurring in our minds. And we let him do it.

By giving Satan this freedom, we fly in the face of Scripture. Paul says we're to bring "into captivity EVERY THOUGHT to the obedience of Christ" (2 Cor. 10:5 KJV). Consider then, what awful sinners we are **in our minds**. Think of the WORRYING that goes on there. The FEARS believers tolerate. The jealousy, as well as the bitterness and resentments. LUST and COVETOUSNESS definitely occur here — in this place where we think NO ONE SEES WHAT'S GOING ON. But God sees it, and to Him it's horrible.

We've got a MOUNTAIN OF SIN in this one area alone, and there's more.

OUR BODIES

Here's a little sin that can't be hidden too well — GLUTTONY. Well, it doesn't have to be hidden any more, for gluttony is now respectable. Eating is the great Christian pastime. People do have to eat, so what could be wrong about indulging in food? Some now even say "fat is beautiful." Gluttony has to be a matter of degree — right? WRONG, and we know it. So wrong, in fact, we avoid the word GLUTTONY. We prefer to say, "OVEREATING." Sounds less sinful. But to God, gluttony is as bad as DRUNKENNESS (Prov. 23:21). Food and drink are both addictive, and to be bound by one is as bad as being bound by the other.

This little sin becomes obvious when the excess weight can no longer be hidden by clothes. The believer may openly profess a commitment to the Lord, but a portly figure says otherwise. A bulging body shouts a different testimony, "I love food! I worship at the altar of eating! Food is the passion of my life!" Satan rubs his hands with glee when a Christian becomes fat. He knows the SIGN OF HIS DOMINION is obvious to all.

Christians are obliged to DISCIPLINE themselves when it comes to food. We live in the land of plenty. Food abounds. It looks so good and tastes so good, **but it is also a satanic trap.** With food so INNOCENT, SO POWERFUL, there's no way the devil will overlook using it against us. All he has to do is get us to eat a WEE BIT MORE THAN WE NEED each day, until it becomes A HABIT. Then he has us. And when the pounds pile up, his MASTERY over us becomes obvious.

A fat body is no credit to Jesus. It HURTS HIM when excess weight reveals the REAL MASTER is Satan. When a Christian's belly rules his life, he's in bondage to the devil whether he acknowledges it or not. He may SAY he loves the Lord, but he loves food MORE, and the proof is there for all to see.

We're casual about this. After all, we see fat Christians everywhere. But that doesn't make it pleasing to God. We're stewards of these bodies as surely as we're stewards of our time, talent, and money. Fat Christians, unashamedly displaying their bondage to Satan, add gluttony to their mountain of little sins.

Imagine, a sin that no one calls sin any more!

TIME

God gives us 24 hours a day. Yet, everyone complains it isn't enough. It's enough for God to accomplish what He wants, but not enough for man to do what he wants.

Someone has said, **"We always have time for the things we put first."**

How about your routine? What comes first with you? Do you have time every day for prayer with your husband (or wife)? Time for the Word of God? Serious Bible study is almost unheard of today, being left for ministers and missionaries.

Got time to share the gospel with a friend or neighbor, help out at your place of worship? Maybe I'd better say, who'll take time? Without doubt, we feel we're too busy for such things, so we WITHHOLD the time from God. Little do we realize how much it hurts Him and costs us. Makes one wonder how He can bless us at all.

The average Christian is in tune with the world via television. There is time for that, as well as entertainment of all sorts. So much time is devoted to worldly, self-centered activities that his thoughts are continually on things of this life, rather than on "things above" (Col. 3:1,2).

To REVERSE THE ORDER, the believer has to TAKE TIME and give the PRIORITY to God. When you consider how many hours we take for ourselves, compared to the minutes spent on our Lord and His work day after day, year after year, it's easy to see how we accumulate a pile of little time sins.

The mountain is getting bigger, isn't it?

MONEY

WHICH TITHER ARE YOU?

Mr. No-thought tithes by. . . drawing a line on the floor. He throws up the money and says, "Whatever lands on the right side is the Lord's. Whatever lands on the left side is mine."

Mr. Planless tithes by. . . throwing money in the air. He says, "Whatever lands as heads I give to the Lord. Whatever lands as tails I keep."

Mr. Keepsall tithes by. . .tossing money as high as he can. He says, "Whatever stays up is the Lord's. Whatever comes down is mine."

Mr. Steward tithes by. . .thanking God for it and saying, "It's not how much of my money I give to the Lord. It's how much of the Lord's money I keep for myself."

Here's a tough area, one where many close their eyes.

Did you know God uses money AS A TEST? Our attitude toward money is a **spiritual thermometer**. The closer we are to the Lord, the more generous we are with Him. The more committed we are, the more we give Him. Inasmuch as God gives us our health and our jobs that we might earn an income, most Christians feel the TITHE (10%) should be returned to Him. It's our way of saying, "Any money I have is from You."

In God's program, there are fabulous jobs Christians could have working with Jesus; jobs which automatically require insight, anointing and spiritual power. But God will NOT USE a man or woman who can't be trusted with money, which He regards as the LEAST of TREASURES (Luke 16:9-12). The attitude toward money is one of God's surest indicators of whether or not a believer means business for Christ. Few have any idea WHAT IT COSTS THEM to cling to money and what that says about their dedication to Jesus. Those careless in this area pile up plenty of **little sins**. Hey, that mountain is getting higher, isn't it?

TALENTS

 "... **When He ascended on high, He ... gave gifts to men.**" — Eph. 4:8 NIV.

Every Christian has a gift (or gifts) from the Lord (I Cor. 12:7). There is no such thing as a non-gifted believer. Talented Christians can be seen everywhere — artists, musicians, writers, performers, administrators .. skilled professionals of all kinds. Sadly though, many devote these talents to making money, building reputations and securing a cozy place in this life. They seem content to chase the pleasures of this world, with little thought of using their gift for the One Who gave it to them.

Then there are those who feel they have NO TALENT, because they don't possess a **flashy gift**. So they DO NOTHING, sitting on whatever talent they do have. Some unknowingly hide it "under a bushel" (Matt. 5:15). Whether a Christian has an outstanding talent or a humble one, it doesn't matter. He is expected to dedicate it to the Lord (I Peter 4:10). If he doesn't, he is clearly ROBBING GOD. When you consider that every Christian is talented in some way, yet note how little is devoted to Jesus, it's obvious we've landed on another area where believers sin plenty, but regard it so lightly it doesn't bother them. It doesn't seem like sin to them.

Our mountain continues to grow.

ON THE JOB

"Whatever you do, do your work heartily, as for the Lord rather than for men; knowing that from the Lord you will receive the reward . . ." — Col. 3:23,24 NAS

A Christian should be the BEST WORKER an employer ever had. Why? Because his REAL BOSS is the Lord. There's a sense in which believers don't WORK FOR ANY MAN but Jesus only. Here's God's word on that.

"**Slaves** (employees), **be obedient to those who are your masters according to the flesh** (employers) . . . **not by way of eyeservice, as men-pleasers, but as slaves** (employees) **of Christ** . . . **knowing that whatever good thing each one does, this he will receive back from the Lord, whether slave or free.**"
— Eph. 6:5-8 NAS

Were you aware that failure to give your best to your job was sin against the Lord? A little sin? I wonder.

To the degree we love Jesus and appreciate Him, to that SAME DEGREE we'll work for our employer. In that way, we are working as UNTO HIM and not as unto men. This makes Him the REAL BOSS. Consequently, when we take extra time at the drinking fountain, an unneeded trip to the restroom, idle chatting at someone else's desk, or taking care of personal business on company time, we're not simply stealing from our employer, **we're sinning against Jesus.** The Christian is under orders to work "heartily" whether anyone is watching.

But alas, many forget the Lord is their REAL BOSS and they can be found stalling, dragging their feet and grumbling. Some even strike. Christians should not be among those voicing DISSENT if they truly believe they're working for Jesus. With their eyes on Him, they'll be content any place He puts them. They'll be grateful for whatever they receive, knowing He will EQUALIZE every injustice on the BIG PAYDAY.

Payday? Sure. Your earthly employer pays off in temporary dollars, but Jesus pays with ETERNAL DOLLARS. So why fuss with an employer over a few miserable dollars, when the Lord will generously compensate you – and then some – when your earthly probation is over? Cheating an employer or protesting against him may seem like a tiny sin now, but it won't seem so tiny when you get your check from God in that day. It will cost you plenty, for your REAL BOSS was disappointed with you. Well, another sin pebble just landed on the pile.

GET THE IDEA?

If you weren't convinced before, surely you now understand there are areas where Christians BIND the Lord with "little sins." Granted, they seem tiny, particularly when I mention such things as: SLIGHT

EXAGGERATIONS when relating a story or event, signs of IMPATIENCE when speaking to your children, and failing to give proper attention to your mate (omitting the normal courtesies we show everyone else). What about the unkind, CRITICAL WORDS we let pass from our lips when speaking of other Christians? See, there are all kinds of areas where our "little sins" abound. And when you add them all up — WHEW!

SIN MOUNTAIN

I felt there was a good chance you had never looked at it this way. I sure hadn't. And loving Jesus as you do, I know you're going to want to do something about it. The last thing I would expect from you is, "YES, GOD, I KNOW THESE AREAS EXIST, BUT I REFUSE TO GIVE THEM UP. IT'S MY LIFE, I OUGHT TO BE ABLE TO DO WITH IT AS I PLEASE." There's no way you would have that attitude. But at the same time, **our hearts are tricky.** They don't always go along with our minds. Your **heart** could well be saying,

"**Father, I'm ready to turn everything in my life over to You — EXCEPT A FEW SMALL MATTERS. After all, I'm giving You PRACTICALLY EVERYTHING. When it comes to tiny little details here and there, I feel I should be able to do as I wish, satisfy my own desires. Surely that's not too much to ask, since I'm giving You everything else.**"

You'd never say that to God — at least not in words — but your **actions** could easily show you feel God OVERLOOKS such petty things. But does He? The God Who sees the sparrow fall and counts the hairs on our heads wants 100% FROM YOU — **nothing less.** Having given 100% of Himself for you, He has a right to expect the same in return. There's no way to get around it.

SIN MOUNTAIN vs. BIG SIN BOULDERS

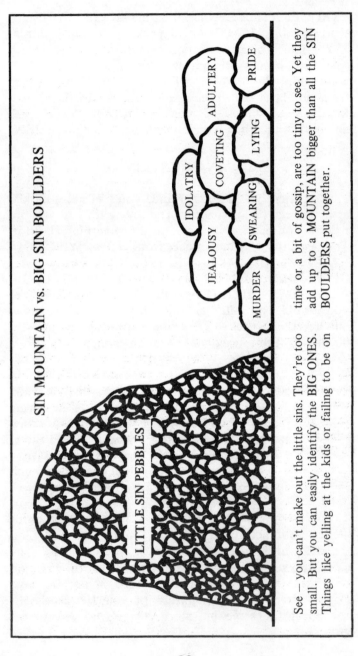

LITTLE SIN PEBBLES

MURDER JEALOUSY IDOLATRY COVETING ADULTERY SWEARING LYING PRIDE

See — you can't make out the little sins. They're too small. But you can easily identify the BIG ONES. Things like yelling at the kids or failing to be on time or a bit of gossip, are too tiny to see. Yet they add up to a MOUNTAIN bigger than all the SIN BOULDERS put together.

JESUS PUT IT THIS WAY

"If you love Me," said Jesus, "you'll obey (fully submit to) My commandments (My desires for you)." He did NOT say, "If you love Me, you'll go PART WAY in doing what I ask." He expects us to yield ourselves to Him TOTALLY, GOING ALL THE WAY. No shortcuts. No compromising. An all out 100% commitment, nothing excluded (John 14:21; 1 John 5:2,3).

Did you know that answers to prayer DEPEND on this kind of surrender?

 "If ye abide in Me," said Jesus, **"and My words abide in you, ye shall ask what ye will, and it will be done unto you."**
— John 15:7 KJV

To many, **abiding** in Christ means slavish conformity to the commands of Jesus. This is because Jesus also says, "If ye keep My commandments, ye shall abide in My love . . . " (John 15:10). But see this: KEEPING the commandments of Christ **does not mean absolute conformity to a set of rules.** Rather, the KEEPING Jesus wants has to do with OBEYING FROM THE HEART. What the Lord is after is a heart totally committed to PLEASING HIM. So please don't think of "KEEPING" in terms of legalistic conformity. When Christians long to do what He asks, even ACHE **to please Him,** and are CONSISTENTLY TRYING TO DO SO, they are keeping His commandments (Rom. 6:17; 2 Cor. 3:3,6; Eph. 6:6-8; Col. 3:22-24).

Will there be failures? Sure, lots of them. God knows that. ABIDING leaves plenty of room for failures. But even as one fails, his heart remains steadfastly surrendered to God's will. You see, even when the heart is totally committed, you can't always get the flesh to go along (Gal. 5:17). The apostle Paul was painfully aware of that:

> "For in my inner being I delight in God's law; but I see another law at work in the members of my body, waging war against the law of my mind (heart) and making me a prisoner of the law of sin at work in my members." — Rom. 7:22,23 NIV

The struggle between the flesh and the Spirit guarantees lots of failures, even when one is determined to please God with all of his being. It's important to understand that ABIDING IN CHRIST does not mean flawless perfection, otherwise no one could do it. Rather, the abiding heart says:

> "Father, I don't like this small sin any more than You do. I stand with You and condemn it as sin. I make no excuses for it. I judge it. And by Your grace, I hope to overcome it. At least I'm going to try!"

SATISFACTION GUARANTEED

Is it possible to be a bigger blessing to God than He is to us? Ridiculous, right? He would OUTDO us every time. What He wants is the opportunity to DO FOR US. But until we put ourselves in the PLACE OF BLESSING, His **hands are tied.** With Him, it's 100% or CRUMBS. Either we want His best or we don't. It's that simple. The moment we are determined to have His best — **ready to go all the way** — we put our foot in the shower. It's that determination that opens the shower door.

Such a commitment puts us on the ROAD TO SUCCESS in every area of our lives. But this kind of success is IMPOSSIBLE without the Lord's help. The world is just too full of traps. But let a person make that 100% commitment to Jesus and he is ABSOLUTELY GUARANTEED a satisfying life. It is the ULTIMATE Christian experience.

> **NOTE:**Small sins produce small guilts that smolder just beneath the surface. You're not aware of them, but they bother you just the same. Get enough of them, and you'll feel totally unworthy of God's blessing, and not know why. Loaded with these subsurface guilts, a Christian has difficulty believing God aches to smother him with blessings. But once he goes to work on those small sins, the subsurface guilts begin to vanish. Then he'll realize how desperately God wants to bless him.

A CASE IN POINT

Remember the lady who put the cart before the horse, who was so excited about receiving God's blessings, but forgot they came as a by-product of putting Him first? When we left her, she had just learned her TINY SINS added up to a HUGE SIN, and that shook her. She saw WHY she was not under the SHOWER OF BLESSING. THEN SHE MADE THE COMMITMENT, and what a difference. I'll let her tell of it:

"I truly wanted God's blessing on every area of my

life, and that motivated me to commit myself to Him, totally and completely. As a result, He has showered blessings on ALL areas of my life — physically . . . financially . . . emotionally. I know He's holding back nothing. Best of all, I sense my lifestyle has put a smile on His face, even with my failures. I can tell He's delighted with my determination to please Him. The joy filling my soul is the greatest I've ever known. It's a SEAL that He's pleased with me!"

If you find the Spirit's witness in what you're reading, the next thing you need is learning HOW TO GO ABOUT IT. With the Spirit's help, I mean to show HOW one commits Himself to the Lord — 100%. If you decide to make that commitment, be assured you'll be bringing God the fullest joy possible. The Spirit will indicate His delight at once. You can't miss it.

Chapter Two

HOW TO PUT YOURSELF IN THE PLACE OF BLESSING!

"He who overcomes, I will grant to him to sit down with Me on My throne, as I also overcame and sat down with My Father on His throne."
(Rev. 3:21 NAS)

When I was a boy, my Scottish grandmother would say, "Sam, take care of your pennies and your dollars will take care of themselves." By that she meant anyone who carefully watched his pennies was sure to accumulate dollars in time. Once alerted to the SMALL SINS CONCEPT, I saw how the SAME PRINCIPLE applies:

Anyone who diligently manages his small sins doesn't have to worry about the big ones. If he's conscientiously working on his tiny sins, there's no way he'll allow himself to become involved in the big ones. Strength to resist evil develops quickly when one consistently works on his small sins.

The Lord Jesus didn't speak in terms of **pennies and dollars**. He put it this way:

 "**He who is faithful in a very little thing is faithful also in much; and he who is unrighteous in a very little thing** (our small sins) **is unrighteous in much.**"

— Luke 16:10 NAS

The Lord says the person who is faithful in little things is **automatically** faithful in BIG THINGS. Consequently, the one who is diligent with regard to his small sins is certain to be successful with regard to BIG SINS. **This is a big truth.** Much is at stake. It's safe to say the average Christian has no idea how his **small sins** affect his growth in Christ.

BUT SATAN DOES

If you haven't been paying attention to your small sins, the devil sure has. He knows the PENNIES AND DOLLARS principle and uses it. He'll do all he can to keep you involved in small sins, knowing it is only a matter of time before he has you involved in BIGGER ONES. When I say bigger, I don't mean you'll start drinking and beating up old people. But he might get you to GOSSIP. That satanic evil damages others for the fiendish pleasure it brings the gossip. Then there are other so-called "nice" sins, such as overeating (gluttony) and being critical of others.

In dealing with our small sins, we can't overlook Satan. He's been working with them for years, using them to keep us from growing in Christ, and out of the shower. They give him a foothold — no, a stronghold — INSIDE US, in our spirit. He's "AT HOME" among those sins.

Because of this, the average Christian can look back

36

over the years and see almost NO CHANGE in his person. Seemingly, he's the same individual he was years before. He's no sweeter. His talents are no more dedicated to Jesus. His pocketbook is just as tight. His involvement with the world is about the same. No kidding, Christians go year after year with almost no change in their persons because of those small sins. They don't even question,

"HOW COME I'M NOT CHANGING INTO THE LIKENESS OF THE LORD?"

NOTE. Don't be shocked that Satan feels "AT HOME" amidst our small sins. The truth is, he's quite at home in our old natures. They offer him the kind of environment he enjoys. The later one comes to Christ, the more his old nature is full of stuff the devil likes. Because of his familiarity with our weaknesses, he can put a lot of pressure on us. Our old natures are like gasoline. Satan's ideas are like sparks. With a single thought, he can kindle a fireball of evil in our minds. The less we know of our small sins, the more unsuspecting we are. This ignorance gives him a free hand to keep us involved with our little sins. So much so, we don't notice that we're not growing in Christ. Because of this, he exercises considerable control over the believer.

SO WHERE DO YOU BEGIN?

Only one place, alone with the Lord, talking to Him like this:

 "It's true, Lord, I've always been concerned about the big sins, seeking to avoid them. But in the process, I never realized my little sins added up to something so disgusting in Your sight. From now on, with Your

help, I'm determined to work on those little sins.

You know my heart, Lord, and my inner desires to prosper in this life and enjoy Your blessings. But I want my success to come from You, as a by-product of my commitment to You. In the past, I've worked pretty much on my own, but now I realize my achievements are pitiful compared to what You're able to do for me. So I am ready to ABANDON all self-effort to achieve happiness and success, and do things Your way."

STEP ONE: MAKE THE COMMITMENT

"Okay, I'm going to do it."

That's what you should be saying to yourself. If those small sins are keeping you out of the shower of God's blessing, then you should be saying,

"I don't see how I can do otherwise. It's clear, I've got to make an all-out commitment to the Lord — 100%!"

But watch out for Satan. He'll get excited now. He'll do everything he can to keep you from a 100% commitment. He knows such a commitment will put an end to his dominion over you. How he hates that idea! If he could get you to commit only 96% to Jesus, he'd retain a 4% foothold. That'd be plenty for him.

FOOTHOLD. The devil doesn't need much to work with. If he can get you to compromise your commitment, giving Jesus 97% and leaving 3% for him, it'd be enough. He'd still have access to your old nature. If you give him just the tiniest opening, he knows how to EXPAND it. Few Christians watch him that closely, and he knows it. All he has to do is wait for an unguarded moment and he can easily increase his 3% to 10%. After that, he'll systematically work at regaining his old territory. Unless your commitment is 100%, you might as well not make it. Satan will get to you in time and void your good intentions. The apostle Paul says to give no place to the devil (Eph. 4:27). So if you're going to commit, go all the way.

As Satan fights your commitment, this thought will arrive in your mind:

"Look, you're plenty committed as it is. Don't go overboard. Go too far with this thing, and your family and friends will think you've flipped. You don't want people at your job thinking you're a nut, do you?"

I tell you this in advance so you'll be ready for him. If that suggestion won't work, he's got something else just as effective — his PROCRASTINATION WILE. It'll come as a whisper:

"This sounds really good, but put it off for a few days. Take your time and think it through."

Don't let him get away with that either. Take authority over him. Tell him to take his suggestions and go. Then you and the Lord CLOSE THE DEAL.

As you prepare yourself to make a commitment, remember the Lord wants everything — every area — withholding nothing. At the same time, bear in mind

THIS IS A COMMITMENT TO TRY, not to conquer. TRY is the operative word here. **You're not going to win all the time.** We've already covered the fact that God's plan allows for this. But He wants you to TRY ALL THE TIME. So when you make your commitment to Jesus, make it all-inclusive like this:

> "Lord, I COMMIT myself to You, right now. I'm ready to yield every area of my life to You – 100%. I'm determined to hold back nothing from You. I'm willing to stop doing, saying or thinking anything that displeases You, no matter how much I enjoy it or desire it. I want You to show me my SMALL SINS and help me work on them as I seek to give You the highest priority in my life. I will go all out in TRYING to overcome them for the joy it will bring You. I have set my heart to PLEASE YOU in every way I can, every moment of the day. Thank You for letting me know You desire to give me Your TOTAL BLESSING."

HINT: In your imagination, see yourself SHAKING HANDS with Jesus to seal the commitment. He'll honor your handshake – if your heart is 100% behind it. That's what delights Him. In the process of TRYING to carry out your commitment, you'll meet with many failures. But that handshake says there's no question about your determination to TRY.

◉

STEP TWO: LIST SOME OF YOUR SMALL SINS AND SELECT A TARGET SIN

Will you see ALL of your small sins at once? Of

course not. So when you are preparing your list, leave room for more. Plan on adding to the list as you get closer to the Lord, and closer you will get once you set your heart to please Him. Our unworthiness looms before us as we draw closer to Christ. This is true for all Christians.

See that woman? She's trying to read a phone book in the dark. But she can't make out the SMALL LETTERS. There just isn't enough light. Similarly, when we're not close to the Lord, there's no way for us to see our SMALL SINS. But once we start trying to please Him, we find ourselves getting closer and closer. The light gets brighter and brighter. As it does, we begin to see small sins we didn't see before. So be prepared to add to the list.

You can't tackle all your small sins at once. They have to be taken one at a time. So select ONE as the initial target. The Spirit will help with the selection. Then give it your best shot, **trying** to eliminate it from your lifestyle. Stay with it, making a good effort before moving to another small sin. This is exactly what the

Lord has in mind when He speaks of overcomers (Rev. 3:21). This is how the REWARDS are won.

 If you were making a financial investment, you'd want to know every detail. You'd want to check on everything before parting with your money. Be just as businesslike about this. Use the "SMALL SINS SHEET" supplied in the back of the book, or you can make one better suited to your purpose.

USING THE . . .

SMALL SINS SHEET SHOWER POWER

1._____ 6._____
2._____ 7._____
3._____ 8._____
4._____ 9._____
5._____ 10._____

My Target Sin Is:

_____

_____

You can use the one supplied in the back of the book, or make one yourself. But be businesslike in this matter. As you overcome sin no. 1, cross it off your list and replace it with target sin no. 2. As each of these sins is overcome, the more you will find yourself under that "shower of blessing".

HINT: If you're tempted to look on such a sheet as too trivial for you to bother with — don't. It will do a nice job reminding you that you're TRYING to overcome, and you mean business about it. Post it in a conspicuous place — unless the sins are too private for that. In that case, keep it out of sight but in a place where you'll encounter it often, say in a folder or a frequently used drawer of your desk. Your businesslike attitude will bring great pleasure to the Lord.

STEP THREE:
OVERCOMING BY DEALING WITH THE DEVIL

When you see your TARGET SIN surfacing — **I mean the very moment the thought strikes** — you're seeing Satan at work. You're catching him in the act of tempting you. Normally, you'd never suspect he had anything to do with it, he does it so subtly. But now you know better. You're watching for him, and you've caught him. This puts you in a position to deal with him.

How do you do this?

Let's say WORRY is your #1 target sin. And now WORRY SCENES are coming into your mind, bringing awful feelings with them. What do you do first? Your spirit must go to the Lord immediately. It doesn't matter if you're sitting or standing, don't wait. **Execute a flash prayer:**

"Lord, as You know, I'm a chronic worrier. It's my number one small sin. I've been sinning like this for years, never once considering the effect it had on You or my

43

spiritual growth. I apologize for that. Now I'm ready to do something about it and I'm asking for help. In the past, I always thought it was too tiny to make much difference. I know better now. It's come up and I'd like to deal with this monster who makes me worry when I don't have to."

You've caught Satan in the act and spoken to the Lord. What next?

It's time to talk to the devil. That's right, talk to him. I mean talk to him DIRECTLY. DEAL WITH HIM. Tell him to take his ideas and get out of your thoughts. When I say DIRECTLY, I mean like this:

"Satan, in the name of the Lord Jesus, GO COMPLETELY AWAY FROM ME right now. For it is written, 'Be anxious for nothing' " (Phil. 4:6 NAS).

Does Satan hear you? Of course, every word. Say it aloud. That will reinforce your determination, though it wouldn't matter if you said it silently. Sometimes you're in places where you have to do this silently. Will he go? Yes — he must. He flees when you use the Word of God AS A WEAPON in the name of Jesus. If you've never tasted the thrill of having Satan flee at your command, you've got a treat coming. Exercising this kind of authority is one of the privileges of the Christian life. Besides, you're learning to handle such authority for a future day (2 Tim. 2:12, Rev 5:10; 20:6; 22:5).

Now you have a question?

You want to know if Satan can read our thoughts, our minds? The answer is yes. Without going into all the Scriptures bearing on this, let me assert the devil has a clear view of your thought life. He sees it as

44

THE CHRISTIAN'S MIND

SATAN | Conscious ideas | JESUS

Spirit's witness to unconscious level

UNHOLY SPIRIT'S ideas are "temptation"

HOLY SPIRIT'S ideas are "inspiration"

BRAIN

The Lord Jesus comes to us via His Spirit. He wants His ideas to become ours. When that happens we call the process, **"inspiration."** Scripturally it is described as, "Let this mind be in you," or having the mind of Christ. If we accept Jesus' ideas as our own, then HIS ideas direct our behavior. Similarly, the devil wants us to accept his ideas also. When that occurs, we call the process, **"temptation."** When we accept Satan's ideas, then his suggestions affect our behavior. Please see, though, the ONLY WAY Satan or the Lord can influence our behavior is **when we accept their ideas as our own.** It should not surprise us that the Lord and the devil both work in the same way. Both are gods, and the devil is a master counterfeiter.

clearly as God does. How come? THOUGHTS ARE SPIRIT. SATAN IS SPIRIT. The realm of thought is his home. Satan has no brain, which is a **physical organ.** There's nothing physical about him. Therefore your thought life is his stomping ground. In fact, **it's all he has to work with.**

If the devil could not behold your thoughts, **he wouldn't be able to tempt you.** He couldn't do a thing with you. Every one of his temptations comes by way of THOUGHTS. He has the ability to DROP IDEAS into your mental stream and make you think they're your own. This is something he could not do without the ability to know exactly what you're thinking. Without this ability, every idea he inserted would be so out of character, you'd know at once an outsider was tampering with your thoughts. He could never operate that way.*

DOES HE COME BACK

Once you deal with Satan and put him to flight, does he return?

AND HOW! The very moment he sees your guard is down, he'll make repeated attacks, trying to wear you down, or make you question your authority in Christ — anything to weaken your determination. But let's consider your #1 target sin once more — WORRY. But we'll connect it with something specific. It'll be easier to see.

---

* Is talking directly to Satan new to you? My book, **DEALING WITH THE DEVIL,** fully explains Satan's operation in your thought life and shows how to catch him in the act of exploiting your weaknesses. It gives a 4 - step plan for resisting him and putting him to flight per James 4:7. It also explains more fully his ability to read your thoughts.

You have a health problem — cancer. This is something many worry about. The very thought of this dreaded disease sends chills down your spine, **and the devil knows it.** The doctors haven't been too encouraging and the devil knows that too. He's aware of your feelings and knows how to EXPLOIT them. He'll do his best to terrorize you with worry and fear. You hate that, because you know it hurts the Lord.

Oh oh, here's Satan again.

You're at the sink doing the dishes when your mind again conjures a hospital scene. Those terrible fears surge in your spirit once more. "Ah ha!" you exclaim, "He's back! He's attacking me again!" This time you use a different strategy. Instead of ordering him away, YOU THANK HIM like this:

"Thank you Satan for attacking me. Your attack reminds me to praise the Lord. In fact, every time you attack me about this cancer business, I'm going to regard it as a SIGNAL to praise the Lord. I'll use your attack to remind me of the Lord's mercy and kindness. I'm going to give praise to Jesus every time you do this."

THEN with Satan listening, you talk to Jesus:

> "Lord Jesus, Satan has just reminded me to thank You for being so good to me. I'm using his attack as a signal to praise You. So thank You Lord for Your faithfulness and watch care. I'm glad my body is in Your hands and I can trust You to know what is best for me. Wasn't it nice of the devil to remind me to thank You like this. It strikes me now that I have nothing to fear because You're in complete control of my life. I'm going to worship You every time he attacks!"

What do you think Satan will do? FUME! He'll grind his teeth, clench his fists and go stomping from the scene. It drives him up the wall to have you **turn his attacks against him**. He hates it when his work brings glory to Jesus, but that's what you've just done. You've used his attack as a signal to praise and thank the Lord. It tears the devil apart to have you do this.

From now on, whenever he attacks with the **sin of worry,** let it serve as an ALARM BELL clanging in your spirit, reminding you to start praising the Lord. It will bring Him intense pleasure and the devil hates that more than anything else.

This technique of using Satan's attacks as a signal to praise the Lord is truly powerful. It frustrates the devil. His big ego is stabbed with pain. Big egoes can't take this kind of a put down. It's the worst kind of pain for them. After a few attacks, and upon receiving this kind of abuse, he'll back off completely. It'll be some time before he tries again. And then he'll make sure your guard is down. You've won the battle.

• THIS IS WHAT PUTS YOU UNDER THE SHOWER — working with your SMALL SINS in this fashion. Your commitment puts your foot in the door, **but working with the Lord to overcome** UNTIES HIS HANDS. Working consistently on that list of sins puts you squarely under the SHOWERHEAD, where His blessings can rain upon you. From this point on, the greater your effort to please Him, the greater the blessings He'll shower on you. Now you know the secret of GUARANTEED SUCCESS as a Christian. There's no way to miss.

STEP FOUR:
REJOICE CONTINUALLY, EVEN WHEN YOU FAIL

Will you fail? Sure, lots of times. But don't let it distress you. No one likes to fail, but **failure is an important part of our growth process**. Many of our best lessons come through our mistakes, our failures. And please don't think of God as waiting to pounce on you every time you goof. Some Christians picture God as waiting with a paddle in His hand, eager for us to make a mistake. When we do, they think He swoops down, saying, "Ah ha! you've sinned again. Boy, are you going to get it this time!"

GOD ISN'T LIKE THAT. He's like any father who truly loves his child. He looks on you as a child learning to walk. What father counts the number of times his toddler tumbles as he takes his first steps? Certainly he wouldn't punish him. On the other hand, we've all seen plenty of fathers get excited as their little ones begin to walk.

It's like that with us. We're still learning to walk with God. And He's thrilled with ANY PROGRESS we make. At the same time, He knows we're going to stumble.

But instead of punishing, He picks us up and starts us off again. The Lord is not distressed by our failures, and we shouldn't be either. As long as our hearts are set on pleasing Him. He's not **one bit** concerned about them.

The Lord is our Father, not a lawyer. It helps to picture Him as a Father teaching His child to walk. It is not the number of times the child falls down that counts, but the steps he takes that please God.

With God, you see, IT'S THE TRYING THAT COUNTS, the effort we put forth to please Him. To Him, TRYING IS WINNING. And with consistent trying, we eventually win. So, even if we take 4 steps forward and fall back 3, we're making progress. That's what He's after.

> **Please don't misunderstand**. I'm not saying God likes sin. He hates it. He knows what it does to people. But when you're trying to please Him and experience failures in the process, He can handle it. He sees the final outcome. Even so, the Holy Spirit continues to convict us. That's His job. What a mess we'd be if He didn't. But God doesn't want us thinking we're failures when we're really not. He wants our eyes on the goal, not agonizing over mistakes.

50

● What do you do when you fail? YOU APOLOGIZE. You tell the Lord you're sorry. And that takes care of it. What do you do when you bump into your husband or wife? "Excuse me," you say. "I'm sorry." And that takes care of it. Things are sweet again. When we apologize God erases the blackboard. It's as though you never sinned in the first place. This is His GREAT PROVISION for us while we're learning to walk in this world.

There's a verse to cover this:

 "If we confess our sins, He is faithful and just to forgive us our sins, and to cleanse us from all unrighteousness." — 1st John 1:9 KJV

See the super job the "blood of Christ" does. God forgives and cleanses us from ALL of our sin. He's eager to do it. He loves to forgive because IT'S HIS NATURE to do so. And He does it in a flash. When we confess, He cleanses. The conviction should vanish instantly.

Don't let Satan put guilt feelings on you.

"See what a weak, miserable Christian you are?" whispers the devil. "Here you are committing the same sins again and again. There's no way God's going to put up with that. You're fooling yourself."

And how do you answer him?

"Sorry Satan, God has already forgiven me. I've confessed it and it's GONE. He says so. Now I want you to BEGONE too, for it is written, (quote 1st John 1:9). In His name, get out of here with that lie and don't come back!"

● You have the picture now. You're aware that failing and apologizing (100 times a day if need be) are part of the growth process. By them we're strengthened. So every time the **target sin** occurs, apologize first of all. God is happy to take care of it. It thrills Him to see you working on it. The JOY He feels quickly spills over into your heart, and you'll find yourself PRAISING HIM and REJOICING.

 "Be joyful in the Lord always; again I say, rejoice." — Phil. 4:4 MLB

In time, that first **target sin** will disappear. When it does, cross it off your "SMALL SINS SHEET," and you'll be ready to tackle the next one.

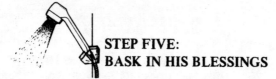

STEP FIVE: BASK IN HIS BLESSINGS

Now for the payoff. Is it worth it to make a 100% commitment? Is it worth it to UNTIE GOD'S HANDS so He can do all He wants to for you? For sure! You'll be telling everyone you know the great difference between living under a TRICKLE and under the SHOWER of God's blessing. Once you start dealing with the LITTLE SINS, it won't be long before you're standing under His shower with a torrent of blessings drenching your life.

Anyone . . . any place who goes to work on his SMALL SINS just to PLEASE GOD, invokes this great principle:

THE GREATER THE EFFORT ONE MAKES TO PLEASE HIM, WITH THIS KIND OF OBEDIENCE, THE GREATER THE BLESSING HE RECEIVES.

It looks like this:

THE TOTAL BLESSING PRINCIPLE

| The greater the effort one makes to please the Lord, out of love for Him, overcoming one sin after another . . . | The more blessings he receives. Total obedience (from the heart) brings total blessing. |

FOR EXAMPLE

See how God's **physical** blessings pour like rain on those who commit themselves to TRY and please Him. He is thrilled to bless their obedience from the heart.

1. BUSINESS PERSONS: Find themselves inspired with great ideas for products and promotion, as well as public acceptance. Their associates stand amazed at their success.

2. HOMEMAKERS: Their children respond to their coaching, their husbands to their charm as they are endowed with godly beauty. Others, all but jealous, wonder how they accomplish so much, yet remain so fresh looking and unharried.

3. PHYSICIANS: Find themselves strangely blessed with remarkable insight to patient ailments, as well as enhanced skill in treating them. Recognition of their ability spreads abroad quickly.

4. POLITICIANS: God needs people in public office where His anointing gives them great favor with associates and the voters, plus more help, if they aspire to higher office. He'll even protect them from scandal and harm.

5. MINISTERS: They build new sanctuaries, provide outstanding leadership, are applauded by their peers, enjoy favor with their boards and congregations, escape financial traps and bring blessing to those they serve.

6. SPORTS PERSONS: With God's blessing, they excel beyond the ordinary, becoming highly skilled. They win matches, become champions, outpace their competitors. Their thrills are multiplied as they enjoy their sport to the fullest.

7. ATTORNEYS: Quickly develop professional grace, the kind that attracts clients and gives them favor in court. They win cases as a result of the divine wisdom showered on them.

8. CONTRACTORS: God's anointing inspires design ideas, as well as unique cost saving techniques. They win great respect from those they serve, because of their committed workmanship. Their fame as honest men spreads quickly.

9. STUDENTS: School is a delight when God is helping. Learning is easier. As anointed students excel in exams, grades soar and scholarships come their way.

10. POLICEMEN, FIREMEN: Public respect and favor

come early. They feel more at ease in hazardous situations, knowing God's protective hand is on them. They turn it into a ministry.

11. INVESTORS: God is ready to bless the investment of those who put Him first. It's fun to plan investments when anointed with heavenly wisdom and more fun to watch the multiplied return. God is happy to prosper committed investors.

12. EDUCATORS: The teaching profession can be rough, but God's blessing can transform any situation. Unruly classes become spellbound when the Holy Spirit anoints teachers, turning them into skilled and entertaining communicators.

13. SERVICEMEN: God can open doors to good assignments in the services. Committed soldiers can look for favor with their superiors as well as safety in combat. God protects those who make Him number one.

14. CREATIVE PERSONS: Artists, performers, writers, crafts of all kinds are needed by God, and not just in the entertainment industry. Those in the entertainment field will be shocked at the skill God gives them to delight audiences. Those using their talents in other areas will rejoice to see their careers blossom under His hand. His blessing is always a springboard to higher levels of success and achievement.

15. WORKERS: Instead of trudging routinely to work day after day, blessed workers can hardly wait to see what God has waiting for them at the job. They can watch for God's blessing as to who will work alongside them, how the boss likes their work, next pay increase and new ways to get the job done. Working with Jesus can transform any job into an adventure.

. . . and so on.

The above list covers a lot of people. You're probably on it somewhere. But will you note these are PHYSICAL BLESSINGS on **personal ambitions.** God is anxious to help His children succeed at WHATEVER they put their hands to. He wants them to prosper — AS LONG AS HE'S FIRST. They can be ambitious and He'll work with them — when it's done as UNTO HIM. This kind of personal success comes as the BY-PRODUCT of going all out to please Him.

"THE PROOF OF THE PUDDING IS IN THE EATING."

You've heard that. Well, the proof of one's commitment to Christ is seen in HOW HARD HE TRIES to sweep the small sins from his life. If his commitment is 100% and his trying the same, he can just about do anything his heart desires, and God will bless him in it. Every day will be an adventure as he watches God open doors for him and prosper him in all that he does. The man or woman making such a commitment can expect body, soul, and spirit to be blessed — yes, even the family. Remember,

With God...
TRYING IS WINNING!

Near the end of His earthly ministry, the Lord Jesus looked over the "beloved city," pining for His people. **"O, Jerusalem,"** He lamented, **". . . how often have I LONGED to gather your children together as a hen gathers her chicks under her wings . . . "** — Matt. 23:37 NIV

As a mother hen is restless until her brood is safely snuggled under her wings, so is God unhappy and unfulfilled until His own are ABIDING in His blessing. We satisfy His greatest longing when we put ourselves in the place where He can shower His blessings and enjoy us every day.

PART TWO

Chapter Three

ABIDING IN HIS BLESSING

"If you abide in Me and allow My words to govern your prayer life, you can ask for anything you want and have it."
(John 15:7 Lovett's Lights)

"Under His wings
  I am safely abiding . . .
Under His wings
  my soul shall abide,
Safely abide forever."

In many hymnals you'll find those famous lines by Ira Sankey. He may have been thinking of a mother hen and how she extends her wings so her chicks can run to her and nestle under them. More likely, however, He was thinking of what Jesus said about ABIDING IN HIM. You hear very little about ABIDING today.

It's just not taught. Too bad. It's the KEY to **continual enjoyment** of God's best.

Once you make your commitment and begin to enjoy God's blessings, you certainly don't want them to stop. You've worked to gain this HIGH GROUND through **consistent trying** and you want to STAY under the shower. To keep those blessings coming and the Lord's heart bubbling with joy, you must ABIDE IN HIM.

"WHAT DOES IT MEAN TO ABIDE IN CHRIST?"

Put that question to a Christian audience and you'll get answers ranging from being saved and going to church . . . to immersing one's self in the Word and praying fervently day and night. While such answers are related to abiding, they are not what Jesus had in mind that night He spoke to His disciples in the Kidron Valley, just outside Jerusalem.

The Lord and His eleven disciples had left the upper room, where they celebrated the Passover and were headed for the Garden of Gethsemane. In less than 24 hours Jesus would be on the cross. There were urgent LAST-MINUTE WORDS He wanted in their heads; words the Spirit would use when He descended at Pentecost. So, as they paused in the valley before a twisted grape vine clearly illuminated by the Passover moon, He said to them:

"We're like that!" His hand was pointing to a gnarled vine that had just been stripped and pruned. **"I'm the vine and you're the branches. Just as a branch cannot do anything by itself, neither can you do anything without Me!"**

I've paraphrased a bit, but Jesus wanted His disciples to understand how helpless they would be without Him. He'd already told them of the NEW BUSINESS

He would soon be starting — **building His church** (Matt. 16:18).

"We're going into the fruit business," He said. "You fellas are going to bear the fruit. I'll BE INSIDE YOU supplying what you need to bring in the harvest. Except you abide in Me, there is no way you can bear any fruit. Any branch in Me that DOES NOT bare fruit will be USELESS TO ME."

This was to let them know what He expected of them. But you know they never understood a word of it — until after Pentecost. Even so, He followed those words with a fabulous promise:

"If you will ABIDE in Me and let My words abide in you, you can ask whatever you wish, and it will be done for you."   — John 15:1-7

Ah, it appears ABIDING IS FAR MORE CRITICAL than commonly supposed. Answers to prayer depend on it. See if the Spirit doesn't bear witness to this definition. To abide, one must:

GET PERSONALLY INVOLVED WITH JESUS AND WHAT HE IS DOING!

Abiding is not salvation. I'm sure you know that. It goes far beyond being saved. It has to do with GETTING INVOLVED with Jesus personally and His work.

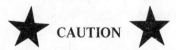 CAUTION

If you are one who has not yet invited Christ into your life; one who has not yet elected to trust Him as your Savior, there's something you must do before the blessings of this book can be yours. It is not possible to ABIDE IN CHRIST until you HAVE HIM. I'm sure you see that. You can't get involved with someone you don't know. You'll have to change that situation if you want the blessing cited in this book.

Here's how you do it.

The Lord is alive, watching you this very moment. He'd like to come into your heart and become your friend. But He's not One to impose Himself on people. He waits until He has an invitation; and that's all He wants, just an invitation. So, if you've reasoned the matter in your heart and have decided you want Him for your Savior and Lord, tell Him so. A few words of invitation will bring Him into your heart — **instantly.** Speak to Him like this:

> **"Dear Lord Jesus, this book offers the kind of a life I want. I see that it is impossible without having You for my personal Friend and Savior. While I can't see You, somehow I know You're there, waiting for me to ask You into my life. So now Lord, I ask You to come into my heart and make Yourself real to me. I am ready to put my trust in You as my personal Savior. Amen."**

ABIDE — AN IMPORTANT WORD FOR YOU

The first two chapters showed you how to GET YOURSELF into the place of blessing, into the shower. But the next two show how to STAY THERE. The key to **continual enjoyment** of God's blessings is ABIDING IN CHRIST (John 15:7-11). Here's why.

No matter how much God showers on you in the way of health and prosperity, IT WILL NOT BE ENOUGH. It will not satisfy you for long. I'm not saying you'll be unhappy with His blessings, **only that you'll WANT MORE.** The problem with health and

61

prosperity is that they are PHYSICAL BLESSINGS. Material things cannot satisfy a Christian completely. He's always wanting more. How come?

Whether we realize it or not, we yearn for SPIRITUAL BLESSINGS. You see, the person inside your body is a spiritual being — like God. We were made for God, designed so that only HE can truly satisfy us. Because we're the image of the INFINITE GOD, our appetites are infinite also. Only an **infinite** God can satisfy **infinite** appetites. Yet, He can only do this when we ABIDE IN HIM. So that brings us back to our definition. See again the two elements of abiding:

1. **Getting personally involved with HIM.**

2. **Getting involved in what He's doing.**

We've now reached the place where we can deal practically with that which guarantees God's continual blessing. This chapter will show you how to get PERSONALLY INVOLVED with the Lord. The next one will show how to get involved in WHAT HE'S DOING.

PERSONALLY INVOLVED WITH JESUS

When I was a little fellow, Grandpa's lap was my favorite place. He'd sit in his big rocker and I'd climb up and snuggle next to him. To me, there was no happier, safer place. I adored Grandpa. At times, I'd say. "Grandpa, I sure love you. You're the best grandpa in the whole world." When I talked like that, satisfaction would shiver through his being. I could feel it.

When Grandpa died, it left a crater in my soul. I missed that lap, that place of safety and contentment. The ache didn't go away until I was born again and got to know my heavenly Father — **in an equally personal way.** Now I crawl up in His lap and tell Him the same things.

62

That may sound silly to you, but when I'm with God in the "SECRET PLACE," I often put my arms around Him and say, "Father, I love you. You're the greatest Dad anyone could have. You're my best Friend, too!" Sometimes I'm emotional as I shower my affection on Him. Then I sense that same SHIVER OF SATISFACTION go through Him I felt in Grandpa. That's how I know it delights Him to have me tell Him I love Him and give Him a big hug. It delights me too.

NOTHING NEW ABOUT THIS

Feeling at home in the Lord's presence is something I picked up from the Psalmist, David. He was a man after God's own heart, one who could say, "I beheld the Lord always before my face" (Acts 2:25 ASV). How did He do this? Ah, he lets us in on that too:

 "He that dwelleth in the SECRET PLACE of the Most High shall ABIDE under the shadow of the Almighty." — Psa. 91:1 KJV

Do you know about the "secret place?" You have one, you know. Every Christian does. It's that room or place in your IMAGINATION **where you meet the Lord.** Have you noticed how you close your eyes to pray? It's to shut out your surroundings — the world, so you can focus on the Lord's presence. You think of yourself as speaking to someone, and YOU ARE. And when you speak to the Lord, your imagination goes to work to PICTURE A PERSON in some form. The image may be vague and shadowy, but nonetheless, a person. That's the way we all pray.

The instant we turn our minds to Jesus, visualizing Him in any form, we're in the "secret place." We're in His presence. Then our IMAGINATIONS help us to see ourselves there with Him in the same room. He's there. We know that BY FAITH. We're there too,

63

and He loves it. Using faith to see ourselves as being with Him DELIGHTS THE LORD.

START THINKING ABOUT THIS ROOM IN YOUR MIND WHERE YOU MEET THE LORD. IT'S THE MOST IMPORTANT PLACE IN YOUR LIFE.

THE ROOM IN YOUR MIND

Imagination Screen

THE "SECRET PLACE"

Where You Meet The Lord

When you and I visualize the Lord, we do so by faith. We use the imagination screen to picture Him in some way. Inasmuch as faith can go where reason cannot follow, it is an exercise of faith to behold Jesus in your imagination and speak to Him as friend to friend. You work your faith when you go beyond that to hold Him in your arms. But here is the FABULOUS PART: what is faith for you is NOT FAITH FOR HIM. **It's real to Him.** He lives in the SPIRIT. Your imagination is SPIRIT. SO what you visualize BY FAITH is actually taking place as far as He's concerned. Thus, when your arms are about Him, HE LITERALLY FEELS THOSE ARMS, Your faith hug is a genuine hug to Him.

THE ABILITY TO IMAGINE

"What the mind can conceive, man can achieve."

You've heard that. Given enough time, it appears man can just about do anything he can think of. That's because he has an IMAGINATION. It is the **ability to imagine** that sets us apart from the animals. For by means of our imaginations we can SEE THINGS THAT DO NOT EXIST in the material world. Before there was a bridge across San Francisco Bay, someone had to see it in his mind. The same was true for flights to the moon.

Imagination is the key to creation. Everything God does, He first sees in His mind. So it is with us, His image. While we use our imaginations to create and invent, this is NOT its highest purpose.

THE MOST NOBLE AND GLORIOUS USE OF THE IMAGINATION IS GIVING REALITY TO THE UNSEEN LORD!

You and I accept, by faith, what the Word says about Jesus' indwelling presence in us. Yet we can't see Him, touch Him or make any kind of direct contact. Even so, we know He lives inside us. Because of the Holy Spirit, we know BY CONVICTION that it is true. Therefore, faith allows us to **accept** what we cannot see with our physical eyes.

Ah, but we don't stop there. IMAGINATION goes even further, allowing us to picture what only our hearts can grasp. Isn't that amazing! Visualizing our indwelling Lord is the most thrilling, exciting use of the imagination. With our spiritual eyes, we behold what takes place on the imagination screen.

When we use our imaginations like this, we bridge

65

BRIDGING THE GAP BETWEEN FLESH AND SPIRIT

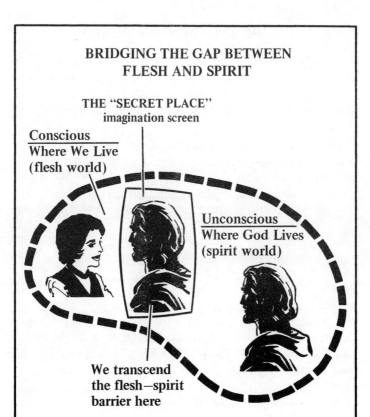

THE "SECRET PLACE"
imagination screen

Conscious
Where We Live
(flesh world)

Unconscious
Where God Lives
(spirit world)

We transcend
the flesh—spirit
barrier here

To test His freewill creatures, it was necessary for God to place them in a PHYSICAL ENVIRONMENT, rather than a spiritual environment, so as to cut them off from **immediate awareness** of His presence. Then He would reveal enough of Himself to them so they could come to Him BY FAITH, if they wanted to. He provided the means for this as well — THE IMAGINATION. By means of the imagination, we can transcend the FLESH-SPIRIT BARRIER and draw as close to the Lord as we please. He is desperate to shower His best on those who will forsake the physical world and live for Him by faith. But to do this, one must really have a heart for God. This is why the faith program is perfect for screening out those who don't really mean business for Christ.

the gap between FLESH AND SPIRIT. You and I live in the world of the flesh. The five senses. But the **Lord and our spirits** live in the world of spirit. Quite obviously, the imagination is the only place where the two **can** meet. So, in the IMAGINATION, spirit and flesh do meet. The poet Emerson understood this:

"Speak to Him, for He hears,
    and spirit with Spirit meet;
Closer is He than breathing,
    nearer than hands and feet!"

PRIVATE ENTRANCE

Visit your lawyer in a downtown building. One of his doors will be marked "PRIVATE." It's for his personal use. He can slip in and out of his office as he pleases. All others must enter by way of the receptionist. In this way he guards his privacy. Similarly, the "secret place" is the most private place you own. Only two people meet here — you and Jesus.

In this private place, you and the Lord share the deepest secrets. Not only your ideas, hopes and desires, but even your sins and fears. Here you bare your soul, knowing He sees the worst in you — and loves you still. Here you can be yourself with Him and feel comfortable around Him. It is here that you **worship Him "IN SPIRIT,"** making it the holiest place of your life.

IN SPIRIT. God longs for us to worship Him "in spirit and in truth" (John 4:24). Men prefer to use church buildings and ornate cathedrals for this purpose, but THEY ARE NOT SPIRIT. ONLY THE IMAGINATION IS SPIRIT. To worship in spirit, we must enter the "SECRET

67

PLACE." Only there can we encounter His presence. There we can pour out our praise and adoration, **and He can receive it.** When you lavish yourself on Him in this place, you are giving Him the worship He seeks. The imagination is the SANCTUARY of the soul. Your body is truly the Spirit's TEMPLE (1 Cor. 6:19), but the imagination is the SANCTUARY (Psa. 63:2, 6, 7). **It alone is spirit.**

PICTURING THE LORD

How do you picture the Lord when you pray? What do you see? Whom do you see? Does a vague, shadowy presence float about before your mind's eye? There's nothing wrong with that as long as HE'S REAL TO YOU. However, we're fleshly creatures. We're used to arms and legs and faces. We like to touch or we don't sense genuine contact.

A person is real to us when we can grasp his hand and give him a big hug. Therefore, in order for us to DRAW NEAR TO THE LORD, we have to give Him some kind of a form, one we can **lay hold** of mentally. And that's where the imagination comes in.

You have to CREATE AN IMAGE OF JESUS on the screen of your mind. You can do this very easily. There are lots of pictures in your memory, pictures you've seen that could represent the Lord. A father or someone dear to you. A close relative or friend of the past. Perhaps a composite of a number of people and pictures you've seen. It doesn't matter. Whatever the source, don't hesitate to use anything or everything to develop a picture of Jesus for the "secret place."

Superstitious about this?

Some are inclined to be superstitious about picturing Jesus in their minds. They regard Him as TOO HOLY, too lofty, too glorious to be reduced to a FORM men can visualize. But the truth is, the Lord doesn't care ONE BIT how we portray Him in our imaginations. He's for anything that will help us draw close to Him. The Lord's not stuffy about this. Neither is He pious nor pompous. Anyone willing to humble Himself on a cross for us isn't about to fuss over the way we visualize Him in our minds.

> **NOTE:** The Old Testament prohibition against "graven images" does not apply to visualizing the Lord. In those days, men made images TO WORSHIP THEM. They were "other gods." But in this case you're doing exactly what He wants – WORSHIPPING HIM. The image you project is OF JESUS. You're simply using the FORM as a means of DRAWING CLOSE to Christ. THAT IS THE OPPOSITE OF IDOLATRY. So don't be distressed should Satan or some well-meaning friend try to discourage you. It is the LORD you're worshipping, not a substitute. It is NEVER IDOLATRY until a person worships someone OTHER THAN JESUS.

When it comes to a precise form, the Scripture says, "No man hath seen God at any time" (John 1:18; 1st John 4:12). No one knows what He looks like. The Lord used a carpenter's body for His incarnation, and it was suitable for what He came to do in the flesh. But when it comes to what he **really** looks like, we'll have to wait and see. In the meantime, we have *carte blanche* when it comes to visualizing Him. Any PHYSICAL FORM IN OUR MINDS will suffice. The way you picture Him in your mind will be as good as the way I see Him in mine. Especially since we know Him after the flesh no more (2 Cor. 5:16).

ENTERING THE "SECRET PLACE"
Imagination Screen in Your Mind

JESUS' PRESENCE BY FAITH

Go ahead . . . walk right into the Lord's presence. Take Heb. 4:16 on faith and "come boldly" into His presence.

SO NOW LET'S DO IT

1. Close your eyes. See yourself in the private room of your imagination. You're in the "secret place."

2. Now picture the Lord. See Him standing there, waiting for you to come to Him. Behold Him in any form you please.

3. By faith, enter the room. There He is, smiling and delighted to see you. Head directly toward Him. Don't be afraid.

4. See His outstreatched arms, eager to embrace you. Walk boldly, right into His waiting arms and let Him draw you close to Himself.

5. Now you can say to Him anything you please. Just being with you and having you talk to Him will sweep His soul with joy!

How do you like the idea of being in Jesus' presence by faith? Scary? Could be, if this is new to you. Yet there's nothing to fear. The Lord ACHES to have us "draw nigh" like this. He yearns for this kind of INTIMACY. This is what He died for — close fellowship with those who love Him. The closer we get to Him, the closer He gets to us. We can cuddle up to Him, snuggling as close as our faith will take us. If you've had a longing to get close to Jesus, now you know how to do it. There is no other way.

COME AS YOU ARE

One thing about Jesus: He doesn't stand on ceremony. He doesn't expect you to dress up before coming to Him. He wants you to come JUST AS YOU ARE. That means overalls, workclothes — whatever you're wearing as you plow your way through this sin cursed world.

 " . . . for God sees not as man sees, for man looks at the outward appearance, but the Lord looks at the heart." — 1 Sam. 16:7 NAS

Men love ceremonies because it makes their importance stand out. But Jesus isn't like that. As I said earlier, He's no "big shot." There's no protocol to be learned. You don't have to bow, curtsy or be afraid of saying the wrong thing. You can DO NO WRONG in His presence. So BE YOURSELF. RELAX and enjoy Him. He loves it.

When it truly dawns on us that Jesus' blood has made us as RIGHTEOUS AS GOD, we can go into His presence, SLAM THE DOOR and say, "Hi Dad," if we choose to do so. Kids do that, you know. We're

71

His kids. When are children cautious in the presence of their own parents? That's the one place they "feel at home." They casually plop in a comfortable chair and start talking about anything that comes to mind. That's the way God wants us to feel around Him. That's why He gave us His righteousness in the first place (2 cor. 5:21).

> **PLOP.** To grasp the casualness I have in mind, just think of youngsters in their own home. They're totally at ease, totally unthreatened. That's the way we should feel in the "secret place." This is the deeper meaning of "Perfect love casts out fear" (1st John 4:18). For myself, I don't always come to God in the same way. Sometimes I'm casual, sometimes I'm urgent. If I'm in trouble, I rush into His arms. At other times, I just crawl up in His lap to feel the security of those "everlasting arms." Then there are times when both of us (The Lord and I) prop our feet on the coffee table and chat away. Some might say such familiarity could breed contempt. But the opposite is true. Familiarity with Jesus BREEDS INTIMACY. The very thing He longs for.*

FAMILIARITY LEADS TO INTIMACY

Family members get to know each other most intimately. Sharing the same house, they become involved with each other's problems as well as their affections and joys. Knowing Jesus as an intimate,

---

* If intimacy with Jesus startles you and you'd like more teaching as to HOW TO DO IT, you'll enjoy my book, **LONGING TO BE LOVED**. There I serve as your escort. We go into Jesus' presence together. The purpose is to make you feel at home in His presence. With a bit of experimenting, you'll be able to take Him in YOUR ARMS and minister to His deepest longing. This Spirit-to-spirit embrace will leave you ecstatic.

personal friend takes that kind of sharing. You've got to spend time with Him — lots of it, hour after hour. When you do, you find Him to be a fabulous companion, exciting and understanding.

Remember when you first came to Christ, how precious it was? You gave in to the Spirit's wooing and opened your heart to the Lord. His love for you was overpowering, you adored Him on the spot. His passion for you captured your heart. Well, that first flush of salvation, that thrill in your soul ANNOUNCED YOUR ENGAGEMENT to Jesus. As Paul puts it, that's when you were "ESPOUSED" to Him (2 Cor. 11:2).

As with any engagement, the passing of time permits you to get to know the one to whom you're engaged. So it is with Jesus. In time, you're astonished to find that someone so glorious and gracious is "head-over-heels" in love with you.

> **IN LOVE.** The Bible mentions three kinds of love: 1. *PHILO* (brotherly love), 2. *EROS* (carnal, sensual love), 3. *AGAPE* (divine, selfless love). Our relationship with Jesus is truly a "love affair" but it is *AGAPE* LOVE, a giving love that is 100% commited to the other. In daily life we quickly learn of the first two kinds of love. But it is an overwhelming experience to become involved in *agape* love with someone. It's so new, so different, that it takes time to learn what it's like to have someone love you that way. You don't believe it at first, but after you've experienced His caring and faithfulness for a time, you have to believe it. Please do not read CARNAL LOVE into our "engagement" to Jesus.

PRETTY ROMANTIC

The Bible insists that Jesus and His saints were

"MADE FOR EACH OTHER." We're sweethearts. When a person comes to Christ, the Lord gets as excited as did Adam when he first saw Eve. Remember his outbursts. "This is now bone of my bones," he exclaimed, "and flesh of my flesh" (Gen. 2:23). Adam was beside himself with joy. And that's how Jesus feels when we come to Him.

Only man can delight the heart of God

When God fashioned us, He didn't design us as pets. He made us in His OWN IMAGE, in no way inferior to Himself. People can love pets, but no one makes sweethearts of them. Certainly no one would marry one. For God to enjoy a GENUINE ROMANCE, it was necessary for Him to create people like Himself — in every way. Only then could they truly be LOVERS. Intimacy with anything less than His own likeness would be ridiculous.

INTIMACY WITH GOD

Jesus loved intimacy with the Father so much, He'd get up "a great while before day" to find a solitary place where He could enjoy the Father in the "secret place" (Mark 1:35). Our Lord was thrilled to do exactly as I am teaching you to do. It was He, you recall, Who described God as a loving Father and taught us to speak to Him directly, "Our Father, Who art in heaven . . ." (Matt. 6:9). The Father's love for us, as well as Jesus' own love, was the heartbeat of His teaching.

Intimate talk

I'm assuming that intimate conversations with God will be a new experience for many reading these lines, perhaps, even most. For that reason, I'm including some sample conversations (prayers) based on what Jesus said about our **love relationship** with the Father. These are simply to help you lay hold of the idea. Once you get started, you'll be uttering your own "papa prayers" right out of your heart. Your closeness to Him will bring them out of your inner being. So try these for starters:

"Father, picturing us together chatting like old friends is new to me. But I now realize this is what You want. Thank You for alerting me to this glorious use of my imagination. Also, for the way Your Spirit makes me aware that You're right here with me. What an adventure this is, Lord! I rejoice to think my visualization of You is going to get clearer and clearer as we spend more time together. This is going to be fabulous, Lord!"

"Father, thank You for loving me as I am and embracing me with all Your heart. Now that I've been with You a few times, I sense Your commitment to me. You really are in love with me. I feel it! What a great Friend You are, Lord Jesus. You're fast becoming the most important fact in my life. The closer we get to each other, the more I realize I wouldn't want to live without You. You're my life, my joy, my source — even my future. I praise Your name that nothing can ever separate us!"

Observe the increase in fervor. This is what happens when you get closer and closer to the Lord. He's such a fantastic person. His sweetness overwhelms you. You actually "fall in love" with Him, I mean with a bond you wouldn't believe. **The more you know Him, the more you love Him. The more you love Him, the more He becomes your daily delight.** Keep it up, and He'll become your **obsession.**

DAILY DELIGHT

Just because I provide some sample conversations, don't feel you have to keep up a stream of chatter. You can sit there and just look at Him without saying a word, and He'll enjoy it. Just BEING WITH HIM in the SAME ROOM, relaxed, is heavenly. Many sweethearts have sat together on a porch swing without saying much, and thought it was a great time. **With words or without words, the Lord will become as real to you as your husband or wife. When that finally happens, He'll become your daily delight.**

COMMITTED TO MEETING

When you discipline yourself to meet with the Lord on a regular basis, an awesome awareness of His presence is the reward. **So commit yourself to spend a "little time" with Him each day, JUST FOR THE PUR-**

POSE OF SHARING YOUR PRESENCE WITH HIM.
We can be selfish with our presence. We want God's
presence with us continually, but we're reluctant to
share ourselves with Him. We're TOO BUSY, we think;
too much other stuff we must do. Consequently, very
few Christians bother sharing themselves with Him.

This "little time" is DIFFERENT from your devo-
tional and prayer time. It is NOT TO BE USED for
prayer requests. **It's dedicated exclusively for enjoying
Him and letting Him enjoy you;** a time for MUTUAL
DELIGHT in each other. If you only knew how desperately He longs to have you to Himself, to get "His
hands" on you and crush you, or hold you on His lap.

IT GETS EASIER

It's hard work to TAKE TIME OUT for Jesus.
At first it's an awful fight, but it's worth it. As you
keep your commitment, subduing the cries of your
flesh, the Lord will make Himself more and more real
to you. Soon, He'll become your dearest friend. But
you have to be faithful, staying with it. If you don't,
PHYSICAL THINGS will remain more important to
you than Jesus.

It's difficult to be consistent. So many things make
demands on your time. Satan sees to that. He'll have
a list of things that SEEMINGLY are more important
than spending time with Jesus. I don't mean just house
chores, but outings and baby-sitting. Dozens of things
will come up once you commit to sharing yourself
with Jesus. So you'll have to CHOOSE a time and stick
with it, giving Jesus the priority. It gets easier as you
taste the JOY of lavishing yourself on Him. He has ways
of letting you know what it means to Him. That helps.
So look at the "DAILY DELIGHT" chart. It's a sample
of one you'll find in the appendix. It'll help you
discipline yourself.

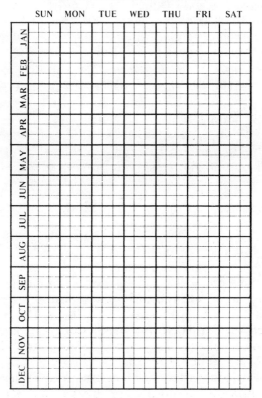

DAILY DELIGHT CHART

	SUN	MON	TUE	WED	THU	FRI	SAT
JAN							
FEB							
MAR							
APR							
MAY							
JUN							
JUL							
AUG							
SEP							
OCT							
NOV							
DEC							

Find the chart in the appendix and remove it from the back of the book. Glue it to some cardboard. Post it in your prayer area. As you KEEP YOUR COMMITMENT EACH DAY, indicate it on the chart. This lets you observe your faithfulness at a clance. The chart gives you a DELIBERATE STARTING POINT, the kind of a tool the Holy Spirit needs to prod you until it becomes a habit. At some point your delight in the Lord will take over and keep you coming for the sheer joy of it.

FROM MANUAL TO AUTOMATIC

Remember when cars first came out with automatic transmissions? I had to have one. It was great not having to use that clutch any more. I could forget all about shifting gears and simply step on the gas. Wow! Did that ever make driving pleasurable.

The same is true in spiritual matters.

When you first learn of the "secret place," your early efforts are naturally mechanical. You have to STOP what you're doing and go and spend time with Jesus. It's so new — so out of the ordinary — you not only have to force yourself to do it, you even have to make yourself aware of the Lord. It's work giving Him a FORM you can relate to. It's work getting used to being with Him, holding Him and feeling His arms about you. But in time the FEELINGS OF NEWNESS disappear.

Then you shift to automatic

When the Lord becomes **truly real,** you cease being mechanical about the "secret place" and become INSTINCTIVE about it. That is, you soon find yourself doing it without thinking. You can be in line at a bank, sitting in a doctor's office, or driving your car. You'll find yourself doing it because it SEEMS SO NATURAL. That's the power of habit.

At times you won't even close your eyes, yet the two of you will be together. You'll be chatting within your spirit. Particularly will you do this when faced with a decision or when you have a problem. The two of you can go down the aisle of a market and discuss what to buy for the family, etc. You'll find yourself talking with Him and doing lots of things with Him — any place . . . anytime . . . automatically.

SHE DID

I received a nice letter from Gail Aggen of Kansas City, describing her "secret place" and how she fixed it up for Jesus and herself. She shared her thrill in becoming intimate with Jesus and developing a close relationship. She enjoys beautiful times with Him in all sorts of places. You can tell she has shifted to automatic:

> *"Sometimes," she says, "when I'm on the elevator at work, and we're alone, I put out my arms and give Him a quick hug between floors. Today we held hands on the bus on the way to work. He tells me His joy would not be complete had He not created me so as to receive my love. And I do love Him so much. He's beautiful, my true lover and friend. Thank you for helping me know Him this way. I'm sharing the blessedness of it with all my friends."*

Isn't that great! You're beginning to lay hold of what John meant by "ABIDING," aren't you? As you and Jesus become intimate friends, it'll be second nature for you to pop into His presence. No longer will you check the clock and say, "Oh, it's time for me to go into the 'secret place' and visit with Jesus." The split second your mind goes to Him – YOU'RE THERE . . . instantly . . .automatically . . . frequently! **Now that's abiding!**

WHAT THIS WILL DO FOR YOU

You're keeping your commitment. As you do, you find the Lord replacing the SMALL SINS in your life WITH HIMSELF. **As the sins go out, He moves in.** The more you overcome, the more you fill the vacated space with Jesus. That's the way to HOLD higher ground. **Satan can't retake ground that is occupied by the Lord.**

80

But if you successfully overcome a SMALL SIN and do not replace it with Jesus, Satan will rush in and put you right back where you started. So, intimacy with Jesus is critical to your success as an overcomer.

When you drop in on the Lord, there's never any judgment in His voice as He greets you, never a hint of disappointment. As long as you're TRYING TO OVERCOME, He's totally delighted with you. How does this help your love for Him? It makes you even more HUNGRY for His presence. He's such fabulous company, you like being with Him.

Does anyone else ACCEPT YOU with all your faults as He does? Of course not. That's why it's so great to be with Him. Even when you've failed miserably — time after time — He puts His arm around your shoulder and says, "Don't worry, we'll lick this thing together!" Even though the offense is against Him, He's cheerful, even joyful about helping you. Now that's a friend — a *best* friend.

SEE WHAT THIS DOES TO SATAN

Nature hates a vacuum, so does God (Luke 11:21-26). When you cast off small sins, a vacuum of sorts is created. The devil would love to regain that ground. However, when that vacuum is filled with Jesus, Satan cannot retake the ground. What military leader is eager to spill additional blood to take the same hill a second time? As General Patton said, "I don't like to pay for the same real estate twice." By staying close to Christ, you're able to KEEP the higher ground gained through TRYING.

HERE'S WHAT I MEAN

You've got a problem. Maybe it's money . . . your marriage . . . someone has said something hurtful. Perhaps an illness has you scared. If you're like many, you can handle it better during the day than at night. Your mind is busy with other things then. But as soon as your head hits the pillow, Satan hits you. "What if this . . . what if that?" Dreadful scenes play out in your imagination. Sleep becomes impossible. You turn over, make a deep sigh, but again those awful scenes keep popping up.

Now what?

Ah, this is when it pays to know Jesus — INTIMATELY.

Instead of stewing, you go at once to the "secret place." There He is. He's not standing this time, but sitting in a big rocking chair. It's just like the one you remember as a child. Without hesitation you crawl up in His lap.

"Lord, did you see me tossing?"

"I sure did, I figured when you had enough, you'd come to Me. All right, tell Me all about it."

As He cradles you in His arm, you snuggle close to Him. Wow, do you feel safe now. What blessedness as He brushes the hair from your forehead and bends forward to kiss you.

You pour out your heart to Him. "What are we going to do about this, Lord?"

"Don't worry. I have everything under control. All you have to do is trust Me. I think you'll be very pleased when you see how My plan works out.

So relax. I know what I'm doing. Just lean back and let Me rock you to sleep."

Your muscles go limp; body and spirit relax. Your head falls against His chest as His cuddling arm draws you even closer. The chair begins to rock. Jesus is humming a melody you recognize. It's one your mother used to sing when she rocked you to sleep. Next thing you know — you're gone. Sound asleep!

ISN'T THAT BEAUTIFUL?

Morning comes. You can't believe it. You fell asleep in Jesus' lap and the night passed without one speck of worry. You awaken totally refreshed. What a fabulous thing, falling asleep in His lap as He hums away your distress. That's the way to deal with sleeplessness. I've used it to illustrate one of the benefits of intimacy with Jesus.

But something else has been happening, something even more wonderful than having pressure removed from your spirit. The Lord got to hold you in His lap — ALL NIGHT. Remember, He lives in the Spirit. What occurs in your imagination is also spirit and therefore REAL TO HIM. He literally had you to Himself all night long, and you can be sure He loved it.

It's lonely BEING GOD and living on the other side of the flesh barrier. Only those who truly mean business for Jesus care how He feels. How His heart yearns to embrace them, and now you're one of them. You'll never be sorry. Just wait until you see what He has for you when you arrive on the other side of the flesh barrier. If getting close to Jesus is precious to you now, you'll surely be among those CLOSEST TO HIM in eternity.

● This chapter has exposed you to the awesome privilege of getting involved with Jesus intimately. You enjoy fellowship with the sweetest Person Who exists. But there's more to ABIDING than getting close to Christ. Even more thrills await when you get involved in what He's doing, and that's next.

SO YOU WON'T MISS ANYTHING

This book has two sections and four chapters. A tremendous amount of truth is compressed into these pages, too much perhaps to be grasped on a single reading. To keep you from glossing over KEY TRUTHS and help you make your commitment, I have prepared 2 cassettes that explain the truths as I taught them to my congregation: 1. *GETTING UNDER THE SHOWER.* No. 556, 2. *STAY CLOSE TO THE SUPERNATURAL,* No. 557. Available from PERSONAL CHRISTIANITY, these 2 cassettes make the book come alive and guarantee you won't miss a thing.

Chapter Four

GETTING INVOLVED IN WHAT HE'S DOING

". . . behold, I come quickly;
and my reward is with me . . . "
(Rev. 22:12 KJV)

About 25 years ago, as my ministry was gaining momentum, the joy of it consumed me. It was my passion. Together, my wife Margie and I poured ourselves into it. Then my mother, who lived in a neighboring town, began to complain:

"Honey," she'd say, "I don't see enough of you. Don't you think you should spend more time with mother? I miss you and need you for lots of things. Surely you can leave your work long enough to spend a little time with your mother."

It was true, I was so caught up in what the Lord had called me to do, I was unable to give her all the time she wanted. Oh, I saw her two or three times a week, but it wasn't enough. She wanted more than that. I just couldn't leave my work to give her more time. So I replied:

"Mother, if you want to see more of me, come and get involved in what I'm doing. Come work with me and then we'll see lots of each other. We'll be together much of the time."

Well, she did. She bought a house directly across the street from the church and volunteered for many tasks that had to be done by hand. That solved the problem. She saw me nearly every day and we became closer than ever. What's more, she was a big help, and that increased my appreciation of her. Later she said she was glad she had become involved. Not only did it bring us closer to each other, but her life was much richer doing something for Jesus. She had gotten involved in what He was doing.

JESUS DID THE SAME THING

Do you recall the time Jesus was preaching inside a house and the doorway was choked with people? Some in the crowd called to Him saying, "Your mother and brothers are outside looking for You." What was His reply?

"Who are my mother and brothers?"

Then, with a sweeping gesture toward the circle about Him, continued:

"Here are My mother and My brothers! Whoever does God's will is My brother and sister and mother."
— Mark 3:31-34 NIV

The Lord was not putting down His mother or

86

brothers, but neither was He about to stop His work for them. That stands out clearly. He was singleminded about the TASK His Father had assigned Him. He didn't allow Himself to be distracted by anyone — not even His mother. If she wanted to be close to Him, she'd have to GET INVOLVED with Him in what He was doing. She'd have to involve herself in His new business.

JESUS' NEW BUSINESS

The Lord Jesus came into this world in a HUMAN BODY to accomplish two things:

1. Reveal the Father, so we'd know what God was like AS A PERSON;

2. Die for our sins on the cross.

That was all. But after He did those two things, that was NOT THE END of His ministry by any means. IT WAS JUST THE BEGINNING. He had a much bigger work to do BEYOND THE CROSS. The cross was simply the FOUNDATION for a far bigger project . . .

PRODUCING A FAMILY
THAT WOULD LIVE WITH GOD FOREVER.

"God is a Father, a family man!" That's the way this book began. He wanted children of His own. That's why He made us. And if I may use plain talk, BUILDING THIS FAMILY was and is Jesus' obsession. He is consumed with the idea of an ETERNAL FAMILY. For nearly 2000 years, He has been SCREENING OUT lovers from the human stream and baptizing them into His family. It's His sole ambition. He allows nothing to sidetrack Him, and those who get involved in this business with Him have the privilege of seeing the supernatural. That's important, for as one beholds the supernatural, it becomes exciting to serve the Lord.

SEEING THE SUPERNATURAL

Rember Jesus' first miracle? He was at a wedding feast in Cana when an embarrassing situation developed. The host ran out of wine. The situation was so awkward that Jesus' mother came to Him about it. From His words she sensed He would take care of it, so she gave orders to the servants, "Whatever He says to you, do it" (John 2:5).

Jesus turning water into wine

Because the servants were working closely with Jesus, they knew where the wine had come from. They obeyed, and saw the Lord's first miracle.

Standing nearby were six stone water jars, each holding 20 to 30 gallons. The Lord commanded the servants to fill the jars to the brim with water and take a sample to the banquet master. Somewhere in the process, the water became wine. When the banquet master tasted the wine, he had no idea where it came from. Then the Holy Spirit adds the exciting answer, "BUT THE SERVANTS KNEW."

But how did the servants know? Ah, because they were **working closely** with Jesus. Because they were intimately involved in what He was doing, THEY SAW THE SUPERNATURAL. And so it is today. The Lord is still doing miracles in our time. Not just miracles of healing, but the way He opens doors for us, creates opportunities for us, touches hearts to change lives, and bears witness to our words when we speak for Him. I'm sure you can think of more. All this is supernatural. If we work with Him at close range, we get to see the supernatural. And when we do, it keeps our hearts AFLAME.

Now that's vital. Because no matter how many blessings are poured out on your life, it can all become HO-HUM. Even blessings can become "BUSINESS AS USUAL" unless you can see the supernatural. Only one thing can prevent Christian boredom: that is staying close to the supernatural. And the only way to do that is to get involved with Jesus and what He's doing.

WE KNOW WHAT HE'S DOING

He's building His church. He is drawing people out of the HUMAN STREAM **supernaturally**. From the world's population He is calling those who will love Him and adding them to the eternal family. But He doesn't CONTACT PEOPLE DIRECTLY. That is, He doesn't touch anyone. Instead, **He uses us**. He works through us. We make the contact and He supplies the supernatural. We work with our lips and our hands and He works by His Spirit. **And if we're watching,** WE CAN SEE THE SUPERNATURAL. We are then like the servants at the wedding.

Remember His fabulous promise:

 "If you ABIDE IN ME, and My words abide in you, ask WHATEVER YOU WISH, and it shall be done for you." — John 15:7 NAS

Those who ABIDE in Him have no difficulty with answers to prayer. They are so in tune with Jesus, they want the same things He does. It's easy for Him to grant their every wish. But that's not all. ABIDERS receive the **greatest enjoyment** from their relationship with Him. PLUS, they qualify for the **best jobs** in eternity.

BEST JOBS?

Did you know that **one out of every five** workers in the United States is employed by the federal government? These jobs range from sitting on the president's cabinet, ambassadorships, department and agency heads, as well as all the subordinate positions, to sitting on commission and advisory posts. Those are the top jobs and there are more than 40,000 of them in our government. Then there are the lesser jobs, those who sweep out the government buildings, scour latrines and haul away the trash. There's a long line of jobs from the highest posts to the most menial tasks. And this is true of any government.

Yes, it's also true of Jesus' government, of His kingdom. He has all kinds of high jobs and all kinds of low jobs in His administration. His is no different from any presidential administration. The jobs in His kingdom range all the way from THRONES, clear down to **the dumps.** Does that surprise you? Are you shocked to hear me speak of dumps in heaven?

PERHAPS YOU THOUGHT ALL CHRISTIANS WOULD BE EQUAL IN HEAVEN?

Is it in your mind that all Christians do the same thing in heaven? If so, you'd better get rid of that notion, because the BEST JOBS are reserved for those who EARN THEM, who qualify for them. Because a person is saved does not automatically qualify Him for one of the top jobs in Jesus' kingdom. It's the same in heaven as it is on earth. If you want a good job, you've got to go after it. You've got to work for it.

 Familiar with the Indianapolis 500. It's the biggest car race in America. But not every entry gets into the big race. Drivers have to QUALIFY first. So there are qualifying runs to determine who gets the BEST POSITIONS in the BIG RACE. So it is with the BEST POSITIONS in heaven. Life on earth is like a qualifying run at an

auto race. You have to WIN your place in eternity.

How well you and I qualify in **this life** determines our future job and rank in heaven. Salvation is free — it has to be. But after that, NOTHING IS FREE. We have to work for everything we get, the same as on earth. It doesn't cost you anything to be born into the world, but you have to make your own way after that. Similarly, it doesn't cost anything to be born into God's kingdom, but you have to earn your way after that. What we DO in heaven and what we HAVE in heaven is based wholly on how we work with the Lord in this life.*

DID YOU KNOW THAT?

You've probably never even been exposed to it. It's seldom preached. For most Christians, getting INTO heaven is the end of the matter. What happens after that rarely enters their minds, though the Bible has plenty to say about it. The fact is, getting into heaven is JUST THE BEGINNING. A whole new life follows. And there are going to be GREAT DISTINCTIONS between people in heaven. Just as you see the HIGH AND THE LOW, the rich and the poor in this life, so will you see them in heaven. Yes, heaven will have its poor.

How do we know? There's going to be a judgment!

A judgment? Yes.

---

* Were you aware this life is a QUALIFYING RUN for the next one? Even today, God is testing you and working with you to get you ready for your PERMANENT job with Jesus in heaven. If this is new to you, you'll profit greatly from the author's book, JESUS IS COMING — GET READY CHRISTIAN! You'll be seized by a new vision of what God has in store for you once your earthly life ends.

"For we must all appear before the judgment seat of Christ, that each one may be recompensed for his deeds in the body, according to what he has done, whether good or bad."
— 2 Cor. 5:10 NAS

If Christians were all equal in heaven, receiving the SAME REWARD, there'd be no point in a judgment. But the Bible insists on a judgment: "So then each one of us shall give account of himself to God" (Rom. 14:12). A day is coming when every believer's WORKS will be examined and he will be REWARDED or PENALIZED on the basis of what he's done for Christ, as the little poem says:

"Only one life
      'Twill soon be past,
only what's done for Christ
      will last."

SALVATION IS NOT THE FINAL GOAL

The great emphasis of modern Christianity, "GET 'EM SAVED," is only half the story. If being saved were all that mattered, God would take us home the moment we made a decision for Christ. But He leaves us on earth to prepare us for the next life. What we do with this one opportunity determines what we'll do in heaven. When a man is saved, HE DOES NOT HAVE IT MADE. He merely has **a chance to make it**.

Heaven is a busy place. God is a busy God. There will be lots of nice jobs for those who mean business, who'll really get involved with Jesus in the building of His church. Now that's the place to invest yourself. So why not aim for a top job, one you'll have for eternity. Now's the time to do it. It'll be TOO LATE once this life is over. "Too late" are the saddest words of all. There'll be **poor** Christians in heaven. I don't

93

want you to be one of them. It won't be any fun, I assure you, for there are no MAKE UP CLASSES in heaven. No second chances. That judgment stands forever. The job assigned you there will be the one you'll keep forever.

There will be high posts and menial jobs to be assigned at judgment. Which will you have?

PERFECT BUT NOT EQUAL

"But brother Lovett, I thought all of us were perfect in Christ. How can there be differences in heaven?"

You're right, all Christians are PERFECT (righteous) in Christ (2 Cor. 5:21). Perfect in nature. But perfect in nature does not mean equality in **rank**. Consider LIGHT BULBS. Here's a 500 watt bulb and a 50 watt bulb, both as PERFECT as the manufacturer can make them. Perfect in nature, yet different in brilliance. They do NOT give off the same light. You could go right down the line to a 5 watt bulb. It's perfect, too, but it does not shine like the 500 watt bulb.

It's like that in the resurrection, says Paul, when we're all with the Lord. He didn't know about light bulbs, but he did know about the lights in the sky. He drew the same parallel in his great resurrection chapter. Note how he speaks of the differences in believers:

 "There is one glory of the SUN, another glory of the MOON, and another glory of the stars; for star DIFFERS from star in glory. So also is the resurrection of the dead . . . "
— 1 Cor. 15:41,42 NAS

No, dear friend, the idea that being saved automatically EXALTS believers in heaven is not true. That's the devil's suggestion. He would lure Christians into EASY LIVING, deceiving them into squandering their time on the things of this world. Masses of Christians are so bogged down in the routines of daily life, they have no thought of QUALIFYING for a good job in heaven, a place close to Jesus in eternity.

SO THE JOBS GO BEGGING

In President Carter's administration thousands of high government positions went begging. They simply couldn't find people who qualified. The same is true of JESUS' ADMINISTRATION. He can't find qualified people either. The average Christian is so deceived about this, there simply are not enough to fill the TOP JOBS. There aren't that many that care.

Consequently, THE FIELD IS WIDE OPEN. The opportunity is tremendous. Any man, any woman who wants to, can EARN a great job with Jesus. And that person doesn't have to be SMART, GOOD LOOK-ING, CLEVER, or TALENTED. All anyone has to do is be faithful — and TRY. Just hang in there, just be persistent. We've already seen that in the eyes of God . . . TRYING IS WINNING! So, anyone can have a high position near Jesus and hold that position forever!

BUT WHO WANTS SUCH A JOB?

We see Christians in this life working hard to get ahead **in the world.** Some even hold down TWO JOBS to acquire more THINGS, which they'll have to leave behind. Others waste hours before a TV set, take all kinds of trips, vacations and tours in order to SEE THE WORLD, which they've got to leave behind. That's dumb.

If they'd take that **same investment** of time, effort and energy, and put that into working with Jesus, they'd be fabulously rich in heaven — forever! That's where it counts to be rich. It means absolutely nothing to be rich in this life because we have to leave it all behind. Besides, we're not going to be here long. Life on earth is just "a vapor" says James. So why should a born-again Christian fool around with this world? Why invest in the THINGS of the world when a fabulous job with Jesus beckons!

Jesus calls us by His Spirit saying,

"Christian, My child, don't you want a job near Me in heaven? I've got thousands of wonderful jobs that are wide open and going begging. Any one could be yours just for the taking. I offer it to you. Commit yourself to Me. TRY, and you can win a place near Me forever. Honestly, the field is wide open!"

Here's the gist of what I've said. You're going to be astounded, amazed and astonished at the RANK AND POSITION you can have by putting Christ first. There's no question about it. A super job is waiting for you, and you can have it. It's easier than you think. All it takes is that commitment and the determination to TRY.

SO GO FOR IT

Say to yourself, "I WANT ONE OF THOSE SUPER JOBS NEAR JESUS." Commit yourself to working with Him. Stop taking your ease. Resist the devil's suggestion that you're automatically entitled to a TOP JOB simply because you're saved. It simply isn't true. If you want the job, you've got to GO FOR IT. You've got to commit yourself. DO IT like this:

"Lord Jesus, unless I BEAR FRUIT, I'm not fully ABIDING IN YOU. I delight in our INTIMATE RELATIONSHIP. but I want my abiding to be complete. I don't want to be lacking in my commitment. So here I am at Your service. I'm ready to accept any job You have for me."

NOTE. As we've said, don't hesitate to ask the Lord for a job. You don't have to worry about being called to the professional ministry or sent to Africa or South America. The Lord is economy-minded. He knows you'll only do your best when HAPPY ON THE JOB. He's not about to give you a distasteful assignment or one you couldn't possibly like. You wouldn't be able to work cheerfully. You'd grumble and your efficiency would plunge. So to get the best out of you, He'll give you a job you can enjoy, one that will bring out your best. So don't hesitate to ask for a job, fearing He might give you something dreadful. He's as interested in your happiness as you are. Even more.

GET READY FOR A SURPRISE

A wonderful treat awaits those who go into business with Jesus. It's one of the super thrills of the Christian life. Care to guess what it is:

The Power of The Holy Spirit!

Did you know the only way to experience the power of the Spirit is by working with Jesus? Serving the Lord is the only thing in the spiritual realm that requires the Spirit's power. It's not needed for anything else.

POWER. When you work with Jesus, whether to WIN someone, HELP him or COUNSEL him, the

98

Spirit does the REAL WORK inside his heart. He's CONVICTED or IMPACTED as the Spirit anoints your words. When you speak the truth, the SPIRIT OF TRUTH always bears witness to your words. The listener may not always buy what you're saying, but the Spirit's witness is there just the same. If someone wishes to be indifferent to the truth, that's his business. Even so, he can still feel crushing conviction. Of course that isn't your power. You have no power. It is simply the Spirit backing you up. And yet, because He is so faithful to do this, it will seem as though the power were coming from you, as though it were your own power. That's the big surprise — working with His power AS THOUGH IT WERE YOUR OWN.

SPIRITUAL POWER IS AUTOMATIC

Come, ride with me in an elevator. The doors close and I ask you to push the button for the 28th floor. You reach out with your finger. Immediately a great motor atop the elevator shaft roars to life. The car rises swiftly. By itself? No. It rises in the power of that huge motor. But notice how easy it was. You merely pushed a button and the power AUTOMATICALLY carries us to the 28th floor.

When you work with Jesus, you don't have to ask God for the power of the Spirit. It AUTOMATICALLY follows as you do your part. The Holy Spirit lives inside you, ready to do His part when you do yours. It's **a joint operation.** When you do your part, He faithfully does His. It's as automatic as night following day. The Lord set things up so that you go first. Here's His word on it: "You go and I'll go with you." Every time you touch a life for Jesus, you can be sure the Spirit will do His job. You can depend on it.

COMPLETING YOUR COMMITMENT

You're working on your small sins, untying God's hands and allowing Him to shower material blessings on you. You're also getting closer to Him as you spend more time in the "secret place". I'm truly proud of you already. But somehow you're not satisfied with yourself. You don't feel right about being on the receiving end of God's blessings without **giving in return.** In your spirit you WANT to do more for Him.

So complete your commitment.

What happens now? Don't expect bells to ring or telegrams to drop from the sky. But neither be surprised if you're shortly asked to participate in some Christian project. I'm not saying this will happen, only that it could. The Lord often takes His time in calling us, but He can also work fast when it suits His purpose. The point: be ready, yet patient. All you have to do is **be willing.** He'll move you into the right job at the right time.

IN THE MEANTIME

You don't have to twiddle your thumbs while waiting on the Lord to put you where He wants you. There's one job, one task, that is common to us all — WITNESSING. No Christian needs a special assignment for this job. The Lord has already laid it on all of us:

 "But you will receive POWER when the Holy Spirit comes upon you, and you WILL BE MY WITNESSES . . . to the remotest end of the earth." — Acts 1:8 MLB

A wonderful thing God has given us, this job of witnessing. For it is the ONE WORK where you can see the SUPERNATURAL most easily — if you're watching for it.

Every born-again Christian receives the Holy Spirit and is expected to witness to his own private world. But don't let that scare you. I DID NOT SAY everyone was called to WIN SOULS. That isn't true. If that were so, His call would be a terror to believers. No, we're called to be WITNESSES — period. And even then, we're not all called to the SAME KIND of witnessing. There are many **different levels** of witnessing. He's ready to GO TO WORK with us and bestow power on us to witness, with whatever **talent** we have, at whatever **level** we happen to be. You see, we're not all made the same. Some of us are bold. Some are aggressive. Some are timid and shy, some are scared. All God asks, is that we work at our own COMFORT LEVEL.

We live in a day when the gospel invitation has been reduced to printed pieces of paper — **tracts.** The advent of the printing press has made it easy to tell others of Christ. A shy Christian can leave a tract in a restroom, phone booth, between the pages of a magazine at a book rack, or through an open car window in a parking lot. It's possible to complete your commitment **without saying a word** if you lack the strengths to share Christ verbally.

Each Christian is unique, possessing his own talents and strengths. What might be an easy witness for one Christian could be a nightmare for another. That's how different we are from each other. This is why the Lord DOES NOT impose a single witnessing method on us all. There are lots of ways to witness, and you can be sure there is a level that fits your personality and your strengths.

A GOOD START IS CRITICAL

It is very important to get off to a good start when you're learning to witness. It's vital that you SEE THE HOLY SPIRIT'S POWER right away. Why? That's where the FIRE IS, where the excitement is. If you can see the SUPERNATURAL immediately, you are off and running. You're going to want more. It does wonders for you to find thrills in serving Jesus.

We are made so that we need excitement. That's why sporting events are so popular. That's why people pack a baseball stadium. They want the thrills, chills, agony, and ecstasy. You can find EVEN MORE in serving the Lord — IF YOU SEE THE SUPERNATURAL.

READY FOR A TASTE?

Good. I'm going to take you on a witnessing experiment right now. The purpose is to let you SEE the Holy Spirit work and experience His power. You may smile at its simplicity, but don't let it fool you. This action provides a very important beginning. Believe me, a good beginning is critical for anyone who wants to be a **lifetime** witness for the Lord. That first experience of SEEING THE SUPERNATURAL is likely the most critical point of witnessing.

So where do we start? Well, it won't be in a church. The Great Commission doesn't send us "into all the church." No, we're going to go out into the world. I know that sounds scary, but don't start shaking yet. You're going to leave a tract **without letting anyone see you do it.**

ACTION

Put a tract in your pocket or purse. If you have some at home, select one that would be good to leave in a public place. If you don't have any, cut out the one in the back of the book. Now you're ready for the first step.

① Stop at a gas station (or restaurant) which has a public restroom offering LOCKED PRIVACY. The door must lock from the inside. If it does not, you won't have the privacy you need. Enter the room. "CLICK," you lock the door behind you. No one can get in until you unlock the door. See how private you are? No one can walk in on you while you're doing this action. No threat so far, right?

Now reach for your tract. But don't take it out — just yet. For a few seconds, let your hand rest over your heart. I want you to feel the pounding. Kerplump! Kerplump! Kerplump! It's racing! How come that accelerated beat? YOU'RE IN THE PLACE OF FEAR. You're in the world, about to do something WITH JESUS. Even with that door locked, you're still in enemy territory and experiencing FEAR. **But that's great.** In order to learn how the Holy Spirit helps us **conquer fear,** we have to be in the **place of fear.** You can't do this in a church.

(2) Now take out the tract. Hold it at arm's length. Look at it. What's it doing? SHAKING. That quivering is your fear translated into something YOU CAN SEE. The trembling of your fingers reflects the trembling of your heart. That fluttering tract is your fear right out there **where you can look at it.** The more shy you are, the more that tract will shake. But that's what we want.

(3) With your arm STILL EXTENDED, bow your head. Prepare yourself to speak directly to the Holy Spirit. Your hand continues to tremble as you say aloud,

"God, the Holy Spirit, behold my trembling heart and comfort me now!"

Yes, you can say more than that if you wish, but the important thing is speaking **directly to Him** while in the place of fear. Talk to Him. Make it intimate. Forget any formality. The next move will be His. He's going to do something for you.

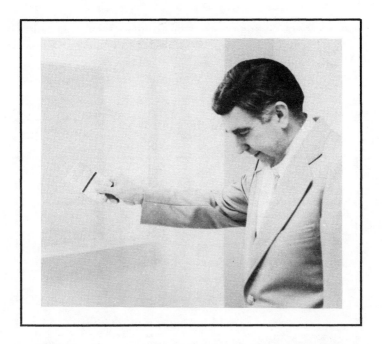

Now look at your hand. It's settling down. Simultaneously there's a warmth inside you. You sense His presence and protection. He's moving on your spirit, making you aware of Him. His presence surrounds you like a shield. When your hand stops shaking and the tract is perfectly still, you are **looking at the work of the Holy Spirit**. First, your **fear** was out there where you could see it. Now the Spirit's **power** is just as visible.

You've asked the Spirit to help you and He's responded. No matter what you thought of Him before, you've now **experienced** Him. You've seen Him do His part once you did yours. YOU'VE SEEN THE SUPERNATURAL. You may have learned the **doctrine** of the Spirit's power in church, but now you've **experienced** it in the world. It is learning by EXPERIENCE the faithfulness of the Holy Spirit that makes witnessing for Christ a pleasure.

4 Now swing your arm to place the tract on a towel box or shelf. It doesn't matter where, as long as it will be in plain view of anyone entering the room after you leave. As the tract leaves your fingers, say aloud,

"In the name of the Lord Jesus Christ!"

Those words are for YOUR BENEFIT. They won't affect the tract any. This could be your first action in HIS NAME — in a public place. If it is, I want you to taste the THRILL of having His name on your lips in a public place. It will prepare you to utter His name more publicly later on.

5 Unlock the door. Leave the room. As you go, check your heart. Is it fearful now? That's funny. Every speck of fear you had before is now REPLACED WITH JOY. You can't help but feel it. You're sure to feel a little flush. You may want to dance or skip a bit. The feelings of delight are so great.

It's exciting to prove the Spirit like this, to find Him ready to bless even the TINIEST ACTION in Jesus' name. Think what He will do and how much power you will receive when you try bolder things in His name!* We have His word on it:

 "Truly I assure you, the one who believes in Me will himself do the works I do, and do GREATER THINGS than these . . . "
— John 14:12 MLB

Wow! Greater works than our Master? Greater things than healing the sick, walking on water, stilling storms, turning water into wine, resisting Satan and casting out demons - and even raising the dead? YES! Can you stand it? Your heart seems to pound right through your chest as you realize this action can launch you on a life of supernatural power — and witnessing is just the beginning!

THE PAYOFF

 "When Christ, who is your life, appears, then you also will appear with Him in glory"
— Col. 3:4 NIV

One day a trumpet blast will shatter the heavens. Eyes will turn skyward to behold an awesome sight in the clouds. Those on earth will be almost blinded by the brilliant color pageant that outshines the sun.

---

* If you're interested in acquiring the skills that make witnessing easy, you'll find them explained in my book, **WITNESSING MADE EASY**. You begin at the non-threatening levels, which become natural for you in time. As your skill picks up, you can try the more difficult actions. Before you know it, you're moving in God's power as though it were your own. I coach you through all the witnessing actions, from the easiest to the hardest. When you're able to move about your private world in HIS POWER, you'll be living the Christian life to the fullest. Nothing will be missing from your commitment.

For there, attended by myriads of angels and surrounded by a host of saints, will be the Lord Jesus — ALIVE!

"For the Lord Himself shall descend from heaven with a SHOUT, with the VOICE of the archangel, and with the TRUMP of God: and the dead in Christ shall rise first:"

But that's only part of the action:

"Then we which are alive and remain shall be CAUGHT UP together with them in the clouds, to meet the Lord in the air . . ."
— 1 Thess. 4:16, 17 KJV

In micro-seconds, EVERY LIVING CHRISTIAN on earth will be whisked away to join the host in the sky! It would be nice if you and I could ascend together, for this is the catching away of the church, the rapture. The entire family of God will be gathered unto the Lord — right there in the sky! Did not Paul speak of Jesus' return and our "GATHERING TOGETHER UNTO HIM" (2 Thess. 2:1)? This is it. And what a moment for us, since we've made the commitment to PUT HIM FIRST and are ABIDING in Him!

Some Christians will be terrified at this meeting, and rightly so. They made no commitment — even though all God asked for was a COMMITMENT TO TRY. Instead, they wasted their earthly lives living for their families, security and pleasures (1st John 2:28).

BUT NOT YOU

There'll be no fear, no terror for you. Meeting Jesus in the air will simply be the CONTINUATION of a deep friendship already begun. This is your "BOSOM BUDDY," the One you learned to enjoy in the "secret place." You'll know Him so intimately, it will be like two old friends getting together in the sky!

As He extends His arms, you rush into His embrace. Without thinking you exclaim,

"WOW, LORD JESUS, IS THIS EVER GREAT! I KNEW IT WAS GOING TO BE FANTASTIC, BUT I NEVER DREAMED IT WOULD BE ANYTHING LIKE THIS! YOU KNOW WHAT THRILLS ME MOST? HAVING YOU AS EXCITED TO SEE ME AS I AM TO SEE YOU! HALLELUJAH!"

You've held Him in your arms lots of times — BY FAITH. But now you can ACTUALLY grab Him and give Him a bear hug! Then to feel His arms crushing you to Himself! Whooooeeee! Talk about glory! Talk about sweetness! After you catch your breath, a huge smile breaks across His face and He says, **"I have a surprise for you!"**

His arm reaches out to touch you on the forehead. Immediately a shiney insignia blazes on the spot. You scarcely believe your ears at His next words:

"YOU'VE BEEN FAITHFUL TO KEEP YOUR COMMITMENT, DEMONSTRATING YOU'RE THE KIND OF PERSON I CAN COUNT ON. I'D LIKE TO HAVE YOU WORK CLOSELY WITH ME IN MY KINGDOM, SERVING ON MY CABINET. YOU NOW HAVE CABINET RANK. YOUR AUTHORITY EXTENDS THROUGHOUT HEAVEN AND THIS RANK IS YOURS FOREVER!"

If you feel like collapsing, I hope I'm there beside you; not just to catch you, but as your friend. I'd love to see you exalted to such a high position, even though my own rank might not be anywhere near yours. I just like the idea of having you for my friend.

109

WILL IT REALLY BE LIKE THAT?

I'm fantasizing, I admit that. But I don't think I can over-fantasize the glory or the excitement of that day. I'm pretty sure we'll be together. Our paths have now crossed and not by accident. We could easily be standing there together beholding the GREAT JOY of our Lord. This is HIS DAY, His wedding day. The day of which He was dreaming when He went to the cross (Heb. 12:2; Rev. 19:7-9).

Can you picture the two of us standing there, seeing Him surrounded by those who have truly loved Him and are grateful for His sacrifice? Imagine how He will feel as He looks into the eyes of all those who LIVED FOR HIM, eager to make His satisfaction complete! I'm sure He'll embrace every single one who PUTS HIM FIRST; and in the process, be so consumed with joy He can hardly stand it. And then to hear Him say.

"THIS IS THE GREATEST DAY OF MY LIFE. I'M GLAD THE CROSS IS BEHIND ME, BUT I'D GO THROUGH IT AGAIN FOR THE JOY YOU'RE BRINGING ME RIGHT NOW. IT WAS REALLY WORTH IT TO SUFFER FOR YOU AS I DID. YOU'RE EVERYTHING I EVER WANTED!"

What a moment! Wasn't it wonderful of the Lord to let you know that in His eyes . . . TRYING IS WINNING! That's what made you willing to TRY and put Him first. And you are winning. You are **trying** to put Him first. Good for you. I'm proud of you. I thank the Lord for bringing us together like this and it pleases me greatly to think that you are right now . . .

BASKING IN HIS BLESSING!

IN THIS BOOK

You learned of the mountain of small sins in your life and how it is equal to any of the gross sins. Because of it, GOD'S HANDS WERE TIED. He couldn't bless you with all this sin in your life, until you did something about that mountain. Taking them one by one, you overcame by DEALING WITH THE DEVIL. It was great to learn you weren't expected to win every time, in fact you couldn't. It's a glorious truth, that, in God's eyes . . . TRYING IS WINNING!

Then you learned that ABIDING IN CHRIST was the key to answered prayer. Abiding has two elements: **1. Drawing close to Jesus in the "secret place," 2. Getting involved with Him at the point of His obsession — building the eternal family.** Good things are flowing into your life now that God's hands are untied. You're happy in the job He's given you, aware that you're qualifying for one of the fabulous jobs of heaven. You look forward to being close to Jesus for all eternity.

Praise God He brought this book into your hands!

THE DAILY PRAYER
OF A COMMITTED CHRISTIAN

(sample prayer)

"Dear Father, I am making it the highest priority of my life to be pleasing to You in every possible way. I wish to fulfill Your desires for me. With all the ability, power and wisdom You've given me, I purpose to give You my deepest love and obedience. May You receive the greatest fulfillment, happiness and joy from our relationship. As best I am able, I yield every area of my life to You. Take me, Lord, and make of me anything You wish. It is my greatest desire to bring You all the pleasure and joy possible. Having committed Yourself to me 100%, I want to do no less for You. May You be happier with me this day than ever before."

C E R T I F I C A T E

THIS IS TO CERTIFY THAT:

On this _____ day of _____

19____

I, _____

do hereby commit myself to TRY to please the Lord in everything I do, say and think. This is a 100% commitment, made without any reservations.

Witnessed: _____
(Christian friend or prayer pal)

112

Appendix

QUESTIONS
FREQUENTLY ASKED...

after reading this book.

1. QUESTION: "Is the Christian who does his best to ABIDE in Christ guaranteed health and prosperity? Or is it possible to put Christ first and not be showered with physical blessings?

ANSWER: God's blessing DOES NOT always mean health and wealth. Some committed Christians never get to enjoy these. Even so, they are RICH in the things people **think** money will bring them . . . peace . . . joy . . . satisfaction . . . contentment. On the other hand, 90 out of 100 can expect to receive these physical blessings. Health and prosperity are NORMAL for the committed believer.

COMMENT: None should read this book and feel God is obliged to guarantee good health to those who TRY to please Him. Nor is wealth certain for everyone who makes the 100% commitment.

113

People long for wealth and health believing they bring peace and satisfaction. But health and wealth in themselves cannot satisfy anyone. Alexander the Great was devastated when there were no more worlds to conquer. Howard Hughes' billions did not make him any less miserable. But the one who puts Christ first will ALWAYS BE RICH in the things people HOPE money will bring them. The 100% Christian is CONTENT regardless of his OUTWARD circumstances — something money cannot buy. The commitment will always bring those blessings for which the soul cries the loudest.

2. QUESTION: "After we accept Christ as Savior and receive the Spirit, why does sin remain so dominant in our lives? Why does so much of it still cling to the Christian?"

ANSWER: Until a person is saved, he has but one nature, the old nature or "OLD MAN" as Paul calls him (Eph. 4:22-24). Having dominated the believer's life for years **before** salvation, he has a big head start. At salvation, a person receives the NEW NATURE (Christ's nature), but it is an INFANT, having no strength. It must grow and develop strength. The process by which the "NEW MAN" grows is through the struggle between flesh and spirit (Gal 5:17). There is a continual WAR between the believer's two natures, and every time the "NEW MAN" wins a skirmish, he gains strength. Until the new man gains sufficient strength, many of the old sins will remain.

> **COMMENT:** The "NEW MAN" does NOT GROW AUTOMATICALLY. The believer has to be SERIOUS about building his strength, much as a person has to work seriously in a GYM to develop his body. He must think about it, focus on it and concentrate on it. He must make himself aware of his old nature and the way Satan

114

uses it to tempt him. He must also be aware that his new nature is weak and must be exercised, or he'll never have the power to say "NO" to evil.

The new man can be exercised in FIVE AREAS: 1. PRAYER (fellowship with the Lord), 2. BIBLE STUDY, 3. STEWARDSHIP (using his money for Jesus), 4. FELLOWSHIP (meeting regularly with other Christians), and 5. SERVICE (using his talents to witness to the lost or build the saints). If NO EFFORT is made to BUILD the new man, NO GROWTH will occur. Without growth of the new man, the believer will continue to be dominated by his old nature to which Satan has easy access through the flesh. This is why Christians can go for years with little change in their lives. Until the new man is strengthened, plenty of sin will remain in the Christian's life.

3. QUESTION: "Why would God regard TRYING the same as winning? Doesn't He expect us to win?"

ANSWER: A holy God, by virture of His own nature, CANNOT set less than a **perfect standard.** Thus Jesus said, "Be ye therefore perfect, even as your Father which is in heaven is perfect" (Matt. 5:48). But God knows there is no way to impose a perfect standard on IMPERFECT MEN and expect them to attain it. It is impossible. But He also knows that giving them such a standard means they can always KEEP TRYING, though never winning. They will keep on overcoming, but never reaching perfection. This is why the rewards of the Revelation are for OVERCOMERS rather than WINNERS (Rev 2:7, 11, 17, 26; 3:5, 12, 21; 21:7).

COMMENT: The apostle Paul was quick to admit he had not attained nor arrived (Phil. 3:13, 14). But he kept pressing on and kept trying. He did this knowing a "crown of righteousness" was waiting for him (2 Tim. 4:8). He wanted more than righteousness. He wanted rewards. Righteousness, you see, is acquired free of charge at salvation, but rewards are earned by TRYING.

As long as a man has an OLD NATURE, he can never attain to God's standard of perfection. But he can try. When he tries, God is at the same time WORKING INSIDE THAT MAN fashioning a glorious creature (Phil. 2:13). God uses the STRUGGLE between our two natures to create something only He can see. The TRYING is our part. The sculpting is God's part. Then one day (at death) the flesh is cast off, and "voila," the old nature is whisked away and there stands God's finished product. You're going to be amazed at what God was able to fashion through your TRYING. That's all He needs to transform you into the kind of a person with whom He longs to spend eternity. Death is merely the unveiling of God's secret working in you and me.

4. QUESTION: "How can God be personally interested in my problems and failures? Who am I that He'd shift attention from important matters of the universe to pay attention to me?"

ANSWER: You wouldn't believe the number of Christians who feel God is so busy with heavenly matters He hasn't time for individual believers. That He is like the president of a corporation. So occupied with big business, it's hard for an individual to get in to see him. Somehow they feel their trials and burdens are TOO INSIGNIFICANT. "Why should He pay attention to 'little old me?'" they ask. If they only knew how LONELY He was for them, how He ACHED for them to bring their little problems to Him. The truth is: GOD HAS NOTHING ELSE TO DO. He runs His universe by laws already in operation. He devotes His FULL TIME to His children, even to the point of keeping track of the hairs on their heads (Matt. 10:30). Unless His children come to Him with their requests and burdens, He is left all alone, neglected. Anything that concerns us concerns Him.

COMMENT: If God wanted pets, He could have made them. But pets cannot fellowship with you. You don't marry pets and commit your life to them. God is IN LOVE with us. We're ENGAGED TO HIM (2 Cor. 11:2). He is not engaged to angels. They're simply servants (Heb. 1:14). He has established this world and put us on it, so that we may know Him BY FAITH and love Him. Once we receive Christ, we're God's very own. He's desperately in love with us, "head over heels," if I may use the idiom. The whole universe was made for us. We're the center of everything for Him. So if we ever get the notion He's not interested in us or our problems, you know what will happen? WE'LL STAY AWAY FROM HIM. We'll neglect Him. No one goes to a person he feels has no interest in him. So imagine what it must be like for God with so many of His own thinking He's too busy for them. **They seldom go near Him.** Consequently He's abandoned by the very ones He yearns for. If you were to ask God about this, He'd reply, "It's lonely at the top!"

5. QUESTION: "When you speak of investing in Christ, do you mean in the same sense in which we invest in the world?"

ANSWER: Exactly. Investing in Christ is like investing in the world. The difference is **we shift our ambitions from earth to heaven** — BY FAITH. This is what makes it pleasing to God — faith. Paul urged the Colossians to do this: "Set your affection on things above, not on things on the earth" (Col. 3:2). He was talking about ambitions. Christians can be as AMBITIOUS AS THEY PLEASE — as long as those ambitions are on things ABOVE. When they are, those ambitions are fired by faith. Every Christian should seek to become as RICH IN THE LORD as possible and do it by investing in Him. In fact, they should want all there is in Christ.

> **COMMENT**: The Lord warned His disciples, ". . . lay up FOR YOURSELVES treasure in heaven . . . " (Matt. 6:20). This was something they had to do FOR THEMSELVES. No one, not even Jesus, could do this for them, and He can't do it for us either. If we do not lay up treasure in heaven, we won't HAVE ANY when we get there. We'll arrive there FLAT BROKE. Poverty there will be no better than it is here. In fact, it is WISE to be poor here and squander our substance on heavenly investments. We use our time, money and talents to acquire wealth for heaven, and that's the place to invest. Why? It is forever! Anything we do in Jesus' name makes us rich toward God, right down to a cup of cold water (Matt. 10:42; Mk. 9:41).

6. QUESTION: "I'm not sure I like serving the Lord for what I can get out of it, can't I serve Him just because I love Him?"

ANSWER: Indeed. But God understands the profit motive. He designed us in such a way that we need motivation. What's more, He's eager to reward us. Most fathers feel that way. Scripture cites Moses as an example of one motivated by what he might receive from God. The Bible says he considered bearing the shame of Christ to be worth more to him than owning all the treasures of Egypt, "because he was looking ahead to the reward" (Heb. 11:26 NIV). Chances are you work for a living for money. Some Christians hold down TWO JOBS to acquire MORE THINGS. Isn't it higher motivation to back away from the world's attractions and invest that same effort in Christ? Sure it is. Many who claim they don't want to serve Jesus for rewards, work desperately hard to gain the world's rewards. It honors the Lord when we work for His rewards, for we have to do it BY FAITH. Faith transforms our efforts into spiritual gold.

7. QUESTION: "What about programs that urge people to send money they don't have — IN FAITH — with the hope that God will honor their faith and send them a multiplied return.

ANSWER: It is a mistake to SEEK WEALTH rather than SEEKING TO PLEASE GOD. The goal is wrong. Those who give, seeking TO GET BACK, have their eyes on MONEY, not on the Lord. It is the wrong objective. Money from God should come as a BY-PRODUCT of pleasing Him. Those seeking to make money off of God are in for disappointment. Those making blanket promises of BIG RETURNS for your gift of UNSEEN MONEY (money you do not have), do you no service. In fact, Christians can be terribly hurt by this. Here is Paul's counsel on the matter: "For if the willingness is there, the gift is acceptable according to WHAT ONE HAS, not according to what he DOES NOT HAVE" (2 Cor. 8:12 NIV). Those wanting to please God with their gifts should give according to their means. If they give beyond their means, then it should be as a SACRIFICE, not as a moneymaking investment.

8. QUESTION: "I am currently suffering from _____ disease. Can I expect God to relieve my suffering as soon as I go to work on my small sins just to please Him?"

ANSWER: There are afflictions which God allows to come against our bodies to GET OUR ATTENTION. He allows the pressure to remain until we respond with some degree of obedience. When the illness is purely GOD'S ATTENTION GETTER, you can expect the symptoms to ease as soon as you go to work on the particular sin (sins) He wants out of your life. Though it hurts Him to hurt you, He'll permit the affliction to continue until you act. There are those who suffer for 10 . . . 20 . . . 30 . . . even 50 years before they get around to heeding God's working through illness.

> **COMMENT**: Illness comes to the body via two different kinds of stress: SURVIVAL STRESS and EMOTIONAL STRESS. Starvation, freezing or snake bite are illustrations of SURVIVAL STRESS. These must be healed medically or by an outright miracle of God. Emotionally induced diseases can be healed by co-operating with the Lord, first by going to work on the small sin (sins) you suspect might be related to your illness, then by working with GOD'S HEALING LAWS. It can be exciting to watch an illness vanish when you use these laws in His name. If you're not familiar with God's healing laws, you'll find them discussed and illustrated in my book, **JESUS WANTS YOU WELL.** The book focuses on the EMOTIONALLY INDUCED ILLNESSES, such as arthritis, heart problems, intestinal disorders, plus all kinds of body aches and pains even cancer. About 80% of all diseases and disorders are emotionally induced.

9. QUESTION: "Could you list some things that would give me a clearer idea of what you mean by SMALL SINS?"

ANSWER: Below is a list of more small sins that **we** might not regard as sins. But God will be pleased if you go to work on the sins that apply to you. Don't get discouraged, just try.

Upset when someone else gets the attention.
Look down on certain people.
Use a white lie to avoid embarrassment.
Not happy over the success of others.
Slow to forgive when abused.
Have feelings of superiority.
Not careful about keeping your word once it's
     given.
Not so honest at income tax time.
Don't mind being tricky in business deals.
Feel OK if your words create an argument.
Long for what others have.
Happy to see someone get his comeuppance.
Resent it when someone passes you up.
Use your tongue cleverly to lash others.
Not truly thankful when someone helps you.
Very demanding.
Enjoy having an advantage over others.
Reply angrily when crossed.
Delight in something suggestive.
Crave earthly wealth.
Put your comfort ahead of a friend's need.
Sit idly by when your help is needed.
Resent being told what to do.
Always insist on having your own way.
Enjoy seeing trouble stirred up.
Slow to pay your bills or meet obligations.
Ready to fight if you think you're right.
Loud in a meeting.
Put doctrinal exactitude above fellowship.
Make rash statements about others.
Quick to pass judgment on others.
Impatient when waiting for a mate or children.
Always have to be first, at the head of the line.
React harshly when your comfort (pleasure) is
     interrupted.
Pass along unkind things about others when you
     don't have all the facts.
Tend to lord it over those under you.

Not easy to appease when you're angry.
Tend to treat lightly any commitment you make.
Tolerate evil thoughts in your mind.
Overeating.
Regard yourself as a clever person.
Jealous of what someone else might possess.
Insulted easily.
You are always right and nobody can tell you
   anything.
Put off till tomorrow what you should do today.
"Holier than thou" attitude.

The list is endless.

10. QUESTION: "Several times you spoke of God screening people from the earth. What do you mean by that and how does it work?"

ANSWER: God created the earth for a single purpose — to place man in an environment that was totally cut off from Himself. It was the Lord's plan to reveal Himself in such a way that man would have to — BY FAITH — believe God really existed, and choose to spend eternity with Him. For this, it was necessary that man be totally free to decide. Freewill has been called the "divine risk". At risk was the fact that some may not like the Lord, AS A PERSON, and could choose to have nothing to do with Him. But there was no other way. Hungry for fellowship, God had to find out which of His creation would like Him FOR WHO HE IS and thus the faith method was instituted. This method is simple:

GOD SUPPLIES SUFFICIENT EVIDENCE FOR FAITH TO OPERATE, BUT NOT ENOUGH TO CONVINCE THE UNBELIEVING DOUBTER.

COMMENT: If the Lord revealed Himself in power and glory, men would rush to Him. This is what men seek. But if He disguises Himself as a Carpenter for the purpose of revealing only His **character,** then men could decide what they thought about Him **as a person**. But even then, God convinces no one about Jesus. Each man must be fully persuaded in his own mind. He comes to his conclusion about Christ based on two things: 1. the testimony of the Word, 2. the witness of the Holy Spirit. These two constitute the EVIDENCE God gives the world. It is enough for those who WANT TO BELIEVE. It is not enough for those who say, "SHOW ME and then I'll believe." God does not convince anyone, but He supplies enough evidence for man to convince himself. Such a person has the kind of heart God longs for. This is how the Lord screens people out of the population stream. Those who want Him act on the evidence and COME to Him. Those who don't want Him are thus separated and consigned to eternity without Him.

NAME _____ DATE STARTED _____

DAILY DELIGHT CHART

	SUN	MON	TUE	WED	THU	FRI	SAT
JAN							
FEB							
MAR							
APR							
MAY							
JUN							
JUL							
AUG							
SEP							
OCT							
NOV							
DEC							

Scripture Text - John 14:6

answer....

THE BIG QUESTION

? ? ? ?

THE BIG QUESTION ?

It probes your deepest secret. So personal it stirs your feelings. Yet what you feel stays hidden between you and this leaflet. The question?

"HOW ARE THINGS BETWEEN YOU AND GOD ?"

● Everyone knows death brings us face to face with Him. And if things aren't what they should be, the idea is frightening. Many push it out of mind until too late. Surely you are wiser than that.

If there were a way for you to prepare for that meeting with God, you'd do it. Right?

The Bible says God offers us *total forgiveness* for our sins, if we will receive it His way. Sin makes us dread God's face. Were you to accept His complete forgiveness *right now*, you could look forward to that meeting.

● Want that? Then take Christ as your Saviour. That's God's way of imparting total forgiveness. *The only way*, He says:

"I am the Way, the Truth and the Life: no man cometh unto the Father but by me."

You're too wise to call Him a Liar. So taking Him as your Saviour is the next step. How? Simple. Talk to Him:

"Lord, I'm ready for complete forgiveness. I know I'm a sinner and I want you for my Saviour. Please come into my heart and make yourself real to me."

Will He come in? Instantly!

● In that same second a sweet peace floods your heart and you know your sins are *gone*. Meeting God is fun after that. And death an exciting transfer! That's big! Yes, this is your private business. But who can get mad at a piece of paper that answers. . .

THE BIG QUESTION!

SMALL SINS SHEET

SHOWER POWER

1._____ **6.**_____

2._____ **7.**_____

3._____ **8.**_____

4._____ **9.**_____

5._____ **10.**_____

My Target Sin Is:

_____

_____

P.S....

As you were reading this book and sampling my spirit, perhaps this thought crossed your mind. "Yes, it would be nice for Sam and me to be friends and develop a close relationship." Most authors are detached from their readers, but my ministry is extremely personal. I use it to make friends with whom I can share eternity. I'd love to have you for a personal friend. If the feeling is mutual, it'd be great to hear from you and learn how you're progressing with your commitment. The Lord might even show us ways to work together to help others make the same commitment.

To learn more of my ministry, send for free information.

All of Dr. Lovett's works are available from:

PERSONAL CHRISTIANITY
Box 549,
Baldwin Park, CA 91706

SINCE 1951
HELPING CHRISTIANS "PREPARE FOR HIS APPEARING'